THE ART OF DEALING WITH DIFFICULT PEOPLE

Your Tactical Guide To Reclaiming Your Power from Narcissists and Manipulators and Managing To Work With Them When Nice Doesn't Work Anymore.

Jacqueline D. Austin

Manufactured in the United States of America

Interior and Cover Designer: Danielle Rees

Art Producer: Brooke White

Editor: Aaliyah Lyons

Production Editor: Sienna Adams

Production Manager: Sarah Johnson

Photography: Michael Smith

TABLE OF CONTENTS

TABLE OF CONTENTS

TABLE OF CONTENTS

INTRODUCTION

We spend half of our lives preparing for our dream careers and the other half trying to thrive in them. Yet somehow, even the most ideal workplace turns into a battlefield, constantly reminding us to wear Hazmat suits beneath our formals.

Every morning, you find yourself going through a serialized internal debate about whether to deal with gossip-hungry colleagues, a boss who is always right, and a group of workplace archetypes or call in sick.

Workplaces are hotspots for unpredictable people. Manipulators, narcissists, hostile and aggressive people, complainers, overly agreeable individuals, silent and unresponsive types, negativists, credit takers, know-it-alls, and indecisive ones excel at turning even the most promising career into a lifeless routine.

Their relentless criticism and constant manipulation become significant roadblocks to our productivity, trapping us in a vicious cycle of drained enthusiasm.

If the above paragraphs sound familiar, you picked up the right book to end the unannounced misery of your life.

After working with 13 different mentors, applying my skills and knowledge, I learned that the best way to thrive in an unavoidable toxic environment is by befriending difficult people.

Yes, you read it right. Befriending those people albeit with clear boundaries.

This book is a guide to help you learn the mental map you must follow to navigate the maze of modern workplaces, side-stepping unnecessary conflicts, recognizing manipulative behaviors, and enjoying the art of work-life balance.

I will also discuss conflict scenarios we often face in everyday life and how to respond, react, or act on each to avoid being the prime topic of lunch-hour gossip.

While the world obsesses over decoding personalities with cryptic labels like MBTI and INFJ, these people are busy perfecting their skills of draining us internally. Your work life should be a source of inspiration and growth, not the monetary source for funding your therapist's next vacation.

Let's change the narrative from merely surviving office hours to thriving at work by dealing with one conflict at a time and one actionable takeaway you can use in your next crisis.

CHAPTER 1: THE DYNAMICS OF DEALING WITH DIFFICULT PEOPLE

The world consists of two types of people: those who make every space hostile and those who endure them.

Difficult people have a knack for consistently triggering us. They are skilled and stay laser-focused on stealing our credits, wasting our time with pointless chatter, portraying themselves as know-it-all experts, dominating meaningful conversations with biased perspectives, or constantly criticizing.

Meanwhile, the more agreeable among us, the easy targets, are smiling through frustration and waiting for a miracle to rip them out of the suffering.

Why do some individuals put up with such uninvited stress? No one willingly likes to tolerate toxicity. The seemingly pleasant colleague may embody kindness, a virtue worth cherishing, but being excessively kind can easily make a person vulnerable and a target for exploitation.

Did you know that excessive kindness can even erode trust? Yes, it's true. People often misconceive it as approval-seeking behavior or insincerity.

The right way to be nice without violating boundaries is by striking a balance between assertiveness and kindness, finding a middle path that expresses empathy and respect, tempered warmth, and notable confidence, which is perhaps crucial for effectively managing difficult interpersonal dynamics in the modern world.

WHY BEING NICE DOES NOT ALWAYS WORK

THE PSYCHOLOGY OF NICENESS

Nice individuals often score higher in the personality trait of agreeableness. They stay focused on maintaining harmony and earning the approval of others.

Every human desire to be valued, but this need often turns into an existential threat for excessively nice people. When the efforts of overly kind people go unrecognized or under-appreciated, they struggle through a destabilized sense of security and well-being.

At the surface level, agreeableness promotes peace, maintains harmony, and avoids situations that create futile tensions. However, nice people are also often perceived as individuals with weak boundaries and untrustworthy.

In a work setting or the corporate world, these difficult individuals typically view kind people as subjects for exploitation. They often feel thrilled in exploiting their harmony through their unpleasantness and uncooperative.

You might think that the other person is admiring you for your small act of kindness but the reality is often the opposite. Here's how excessively nice people are often perceived in a corporate setting or any working environment.

Weak Boundaries: Excessive niceness often signals non-existent or negotiable boundaries, making such individuals an easy target to fall prey to difficult people. Manipulators exploit this trait by pushing boundaries, knowing that the person will eventually yield to avoid unnecessary conflict.

Assumption of Compliance: Agreeable people frequently find themselves in situations that they never agreed upon. These people are often susceptible to overloaded tasks and un-credited projects because they rarely refuse requests. This creates an expectation of compliance, allowing others to assert dominance.

Expulsion of Authenticity: While being nice may bring you short-term benefits, authenticity garners respect and value. If you are someone who agrees with every opinion or decision, you would rather be perceived as insincere, and considered as a person with a lack of judgment, leading to lesser respect. Difficult people take advantage of this trait and view it as an invitation to manipulation and exploitation during conflicts, discussions, and negotiations.

ASSERTIVENESS VS. AGREEABLENESS

There is a stark difference between being assertive in your responses and simply acquiescing to every tantrum thrown at you. The solution lies in learning the key difference between both. Recognizing the difference will also help you avoid situations that exploit and ruin your inner peace.

Being Agreeable means prioritizing harmony and avoiding every possible conflict, be it constructive or unconstructive, often at the expense of violating your own personal boundaries and needs.

GOAL: To avoid conflict.

OUTCOME: Short-term peace but long-term resentment.

EXAMPLE: Letting a colleague take credit for a project even when they hardly contributed, shouldering unnecessary workloads, or fixing others' mistakes silently without informing or highlighting them to the doer.

On the other hand,

Assertiveness emphasizes setting clear boundaries and fostering respectful communication that addresses the needs of all parties.

GOAL: Build and foster honest interaction with mutual respect.

OUTCOME: Strong, healthier work relationships, even if initial tensions arise.

EXAMPLE: Politely declining unreasonable requests, saying 'no' to uncalled favors, or logically explaining why a criticism is unwarranted.

Assertiveness helps to build and nurture clear personal boundaries without aggression or suppressed resentment. It strikes a balance between passivity and confrontation, allowing you to handle and deal with difficult personalities effectively.

SOCIETAL EXPECTATIONS AND CONFLICT AVOIDANCE

When we were children, we often made choices that benefitted us solely. The need to appear kind, share our belongings, and consider other people's perspectives arises when we learn difficult words like selfish, mean, and unreliable.

These words were necessary to complete and shape our personality trait set. However, although lessons on *how to become a nice individual when you grow up* were well-intentioned, it often backfired for many of us.

Consequently, a series of forced sacrifices and hiding beneath happy masks to be loved and accepted by everyone became our second nature.

There are specific societal expectations and a deep-rooted aversion to conflict that excessively kind individuals feel compelled to follow, often at the cost of going beyond personal boundaries to seek the approval of others and end up encouraging a lifelong habit of avoiding confrontation.

Some of the societal expectations that stem from conflict avoidance are:

1. The Fear of Being Disliked or Labeled as Being Difficult:

Generally, women are perceived as unlikeable when they share strong contrasting opinions. As a result, they often lie low in a professional setting to maintain harmony and avoid being seen as confrontational.

2. The Constant Desire to Avoid Confrontation:

Confrontations involve emotional vulnerability, exposure to unaltered feelings, and the fear of being judged and criticized by others, which can feel risky in unfavorable environments.

To avoid such unnecessary remarks, individuals often act excessively kind, which may act as a shield against conflicts. However, this technique is counterproductive as it leaves individuals with deeper unresolved issues and grudges over futile matters.

3. Cultural Differences:

Cultural norms shape our perception of niceness. People born and brought up in different countries, cultures, religions, or even the same families often hold different definitions of kindness and being nice to others.

This kind of diversification in a workplace often makes it more challenging to address difficult situations firmly. Navigating these differences in a workplace requires humility and polite communication to avoid conflicts over respect or morality.

REEVALUATING NICENESS THROUGH BOUNDARIES

Being nice isn't a flaw. It is not a condition that needs to be remedied. Having a personality that is considered nice or kind becomes problematic only when personal boundaries are compromised. To balance your assertiveness and kindness, you must express your sincere opinions to others. Here are three simple steps that help you channel your assertiveness.

- **Speak Up When Necessary:** Instead of passively agreeing, use a polite but firm tone in listing the differences between yours and the opinions of others. Analyze every point through three or more perspectives- advantages of agreeing to the proposal, disadvantages of agreeing to the proposal, and dismissing or being neutral. Weigh out the consequences of each analysis and create a conclusion that favors the needs of both parties.

- **Set Clear Boundaries:** If you are deciding to help someone else in their work or taking on an extra workload, make sure to highlight your kind gesture through phrases like;

'It was a pleasure to assist you in this task, but it would be beneficial if we could plan better next time to avoid last-minute adjustments.'

'I'm happy to contribute to your project, but I'd need your input on X to make it more efficient.'

'I'll be glad to help you, but I'd like us to discuss re-distributing some responsibilities in the future to ensure balance and avoid being in a time crunch.'

Phrases like these are excellent in portraying your willingness to help and setting up an expectation for accountability and fairness. You can use these phrases after the completion of a project or before by reading the room and the criticality of the project.

Clear communication is an effective way to set boundaries and establish professional respect. It further ensures that your efforts are recognized as exceptional rather than expected.

- **Stop Avoiding Issues:** The secret to building healthier relationships is not by avoiding but by confronting challenges. Conflicts in relationships are as natural as siblings disagreeing to eat similar foods.

Confronting issues may put you in short-term disagreement. But in the long run, it further helps you to release suppressed anger and bitterness and cease building up new reasons for tensions or conflicts.

HOW TO DIFFERENTIATE BETWEEN HOT AND COLD CONFLICT CREATORS

There are two types of conflict creators in this world; hot conflict creators and cold conflict creators. According to Mark Gerzon, the author of *'Dealing with Difficult People'*, companies, educational institutions, and faith-based organizations are prone to cold conflicts whereas politicians often engage in hot conflicts.

Conflicts instigated by cold conflict creators are challenging to navigate as they often leave pressing issues unaddressed and concerns unexpressed.

On the other hand, conflicts initiated by hot conflict creators are often marked by hostility, aggression, and abusive tactics, whether physical or emotional, escalating tensions, jeopardizing agreements and potentially severing favorable professional relationships.

An effective way to deal with the combative duo is by answering a simple question of whether the conflict is created by a hot conflict creator or a cold conflict creator. Once you have your answer, you can easily analyze the situation and create a resolution as per the outcome.

To help you quickly analyze the trait of the conflict creator, here are some behaviors that the duo showcases:

Hot Conflict Creators: Highly emotionally expressive, speak loudly or shout at every disagreement to be heard, physically aggressive, wild, or threatening even for trivial issues, prefers to use incendiary language, appears out of control and potentially explosive.

Cold Conflict Creators: Suppress emotions that must be expressed, mutter under their breath to avoid further confrontation, purse their lips or be physically withdrawn from the conversations, turn away or avoid contact, remain silent or reply in a passive-aggressive way, and appear distant and uninterested.

Understanding and identifying the traits and behaviors of conflict creators is essential as it helps to set the ground rules for a favorable resolution.

HOW TO DEAL WITH HOT CONFLICT CREATORS

If both participants are hot conflict creators, consider setting ground rules to control the explosive nature of both parties before giving them the chance to speak. Hot conflict creators escalate trivial matters into heated arguments within seconds.

They possess an ability to escalate minor disagreements into full-blown conflicts rapidly. The best way to deal with these kinds of hot conflict creators is through de-escalation, regulating the temperature gauge of the conversations to diffuse tension.

Here are three simple approaches to effectively deal with hot conflict creators:

Set a Time Limit: Consider setting a time limit for each participant in the debate. Giving equal time to both parties to express their concerns individually fosters equal opportunity, encourages active participation, and eliminates any sense of favoritism and bias.

Begin The Conversation with a Reflective Question: Reflective questions like; *'Why do you believe your approach is* *an effective way to resolve this conflict while engaging others?' or 'How are you managing to maintain work-life balance with the recent changes in the procedure'* shifts the conversation from blame to understating each individual's perspective. It also makes discussions more empathetic and constructive.

Focus on Building Trust Gradually: When you ask a thoughtful question that helps participants understand each other's viewpoints, it fosters trust and mutual respect, making it easier to address and tackle challenging issues easily over time.

HOW TO DEAL WITH COLD CONFLICT CREATORS

When dealing with cold conflict creators, focus on creating an environment that encourages them to speak. Cold conflict creators are passive-aggressive and extremely reserved. They may silently harbor a strong resentment throughout their lives rather than confronting the issue upfront. Encouraging and motivating them to express and share their concerns without fearing offense or judgment is an effective way to warm up the conflicts.

The three strategies that could help in melting the ice of cold conflicts are:

Hold a Debate Session: If one or more groups avoid discussing critical issues impacting the entire project, organize a structured group debate. Encourage participation by giving each individual an opportunity to speak. This approach further helps uncover underlying issues, promotes open communication, and prevents unresolved conflicts from escalating.

Stay Alert or Be Present: When an issue is addressed between two cold conflict creators, oftentimes, the participants withdraw themselves or turn hostile towards each other. To navigate thoughtfully in such situations, try to steer the discussion towards open-ended topics. This method fosters mutual understanding and facilitates meaningful dialogues to manage and channel suppressed emotions.

Use Structured Debates: Structured debates are a great tool to exercise constructive criticism and accentuate differences of opinions in a controlled and productive manner. Choose topics that encourage and shift focus on addressing underlying issues to resolve the un-verbalized bitterness.

In cold and hot conflicts, focus on bridging the differences of both parties to create solutions driven towards a common goal. Don't rush decisions, and take time to evaluate every suggestion. Listen attentively but respond selectively to avoid appearing offensive or diminishing. If you find the conflict challenging or struggle to establish a common ground between both parties, reach out and include a third party as a neutral observer. Including an outsider

encourages unbiased perspectives and inspires fresh, innovative resolutions.

CASE STUDY

A finance department employee, **John**, often feels underappreciated because his ideas for improving the budgeting process have gone unnoticed for several months. Instead of voicing his concerns, he mutters under his breath during team meetings and stares at team members with a cold gaze, creating a tense atmosphere.

On the other hand, **Emily**, a marketing team employee, often lashes out under the constant pressure of tight campaign deadlines, even when minor hiccups occur, such as delayed reports from John's team.

David, their supervisor, notices the conflict and steps in. During a team meeting, David observes Emily's frustration over the pressing issues and John's dismissive remarks about the project. To resolve this, he schedules one-on-one conversations with each of them.

For John: David acknowledges his frustrations, asks for details about his ideas, suggests ways to present his ideas to the appropriate authorities, and assures him that his input will be considered in future planning sessions.

For Emily: David empathizes with her stress, suggests time management strategies, and reinforces the importance of communicating calmly in stressful situations.

Then, David brings them together in a neutral setting. Instead of taking sides, he focuses on fostering team collaboration by:

- **Highlighting Shared Goals:** David redirects the conversation by reminding them of the main objective and how both of their opinions are necessary to make a successful campaign with effective budgeting.

- **Providing Options:** He proposes a strategic workflow by requesting John's team to submit their reports one day earlier. This approach gives Emily's team enough time to act on them and avoid last-minute errors.

- **Encouraging Feedback:** David creates a safe space by being neutral to both parties, helping them share remarks, openly discussing concerns, and agreeing on practical solutions.

By facilitating a simple approach, David diffuses unnecessary tension. John feels heard, and Emily learns to manage stress, making the team work effectively on the campaign. The first campaign becomes a foundation for growing mutual respect and trust, making future collaboration smoother and less stressful for everyone.

IDENTIFYING & UNDERSTANDING PERSONAL TRIGGERS IN DEALING WITH CONFLICTS

RECOGNIZING YOUR BODY'S ALARM SYSTEM

Triggers act as switches that activate a response, like setting a device into motion. Once flipped, they create a chain reaction affecting your thoughts, behaviors, and actions. When our surroundings provoke a trigger, the brain sends signals to the body, initiating a response to address the perceived situation. It commands the body to fight the potential threat.

When someone says they are triggered by a situation or a person, view it as the body's internal protective mechanism rather than dismissing or belittling it.

Triggers are as common as the person who sits next to you. Understanding and identifying personal triggers can help individuals and organizations implement strategies to diminish their impact, promote healthier work environments, and support employees to become more productive.

Personal triggers are shaped and influenced by an individual's preferred lifestyle choices, beliefs, upbringing, past experiences, trauma, dreams, personal goals, habits, and behavior. Workplace triggers can stem from various sources and affect us differently based on our emotional response to the triggering situation. Some of the most common triggers faced by every working individual include:

✓ Deadline Pressure

✓ Micromanagement

✓ Workload Imbalance

✓ Lack of Recognition or Appreciation

✓ Feedback Criticism

✓ Changes in Routines or Procedures

✓ Inadequate Resources or Support

✓ Challenges in Work-Life Balance

Handling these work triggers requires a proactive approach. It often involves a combination of personal strategies, communication skills, and seeking external support whenever necessary. Have an honest conversation with yourself. Building resilience begins with understanding yourself better and how each trigger affects your growth and mindset. Reaching out for external support often is the best way to minimize the impact of each trigger.

Here are some powerful proactive techniques to deal with each kind of trigger in the workplace:

✓ **Deadline Pressure:** Tight Deadlines overwhelm us with unrealistic expectations and trigger a sense of urgency that further affects our decision-making ability and productivity. Completing projects on time is crucial for any organization and sector. Meeting deadlines ensures efficiency, maintains client satisfaction, and upholds the company's reputation. However, agreeing to unrealistic timelines without clear communication often leads to unnecessary tension.

Here are some actionable steps to help you manage tight deadlines.

Communicate Your Needs Clearly During Project Assignment

When assigned to a new project, it's common to agree to every demand without analyzing the resources, time, and materials required. However, it's essential to set realistic expectations right from the beginning of the project to avoid unnecessary tension. Communicate your needs clearly and effectively using phrases like, *"I'll do my best to meet the deadline. However, after initial research, I'll reassess and confirm the feasibility."*

Avoid waiting until the last moment to voice concerns and update stakeholders about your progress and potential challenges. This also highlights how proactively you are working on the assigned task, which further aligns you to better future opportunities.

If faced with unrealistic deadlines, address the issue promptly. Clearly outline the time and effort required to deliver quality results and suggest alternative timelines or solutions to ensure project success.

Utilize Time Management Techniques

Instead of tackling the entire project in one go, divide it into manageable sections. Create time blocks to dedicate required hours for each phase and adjust according to resource availability, project demands, and team requirements.

Define clear objectives and set actionable goals with a realistic timeline. For example; if your team is assigned to develop a new app, analyze your team's strengths and weaknesses and assign specific hours for each task such as interface designing, coding, trial tests, feature enhancement, etc.

While organizing the project, create a structured routine to handle built-in buffers to account for unexpected delays. Use collaboration tools and project management platforms to keep all team members informed and updated about recent changes.

Involving each team member ensures alignment, minimizes future miscommunication and project delays. Similarly, creating a contingency plan that outlines an alternative approach protects you from uncalled setbacks.

Address Issues Promptly

Try to nurture an environment where team members feel comfortable and heard while voicing their concerns as soon as they arise. Create a safe space by approaching challenges calmly and constructively. Take immediate action rather than delaying issues and leaving individuals to struggle alone.

Acting promptly to resolve issues saves time and prevents delays or setbacks that could hinder progress. Encouraging transparency and collaboration ensures a smoother workflow and stronger team cohesion.

✓ **Micromanagement:** Feeling like someone is watching your every move at work can be incredibly draining. Being excessively monitored for every minute of the project or work creates a sense of mistrust, lack of autonomy, and decreased morale. You will often be stifled at making decisions and question your abilities. Productivity varies among individuals. Some people thrive under mentorship, while others excel at operating independently. Your authentic leadership qualities involve recognizing each team member's working preferences, pairing individuals whose strengths complement each other for optimal collaboration, and keeping the projects moving forward easily.

If you are dealing with a micromanaging boss, mentor, or senior, one of the best ways to ease the tension is to get ahead of it. Proactively share your progress, and keep everyone updated in your team, communicate clearly about the difficulties and challenges you are facing. This tactic further reduces the need for constant check-ins, project anxiety, and decision paralysis. Offer thoughtful suggestions and solutions to demonstrate your competence and build trust, creating a more empowered and productive work environment.

✓ **Workload Imbalance:** Agreeing to every task assigned, primarily beyond work hours or your defined responsibilities, only leads to burnout and hinders your ability to seize better opportunities. Occasionally, taking an extra task to support a colleague or meeting tight deadlines shows teamwork and makes you appear reliable. But it's essential for you to set boundaries if this becomes an ongoing expectation.

Unclear communication can lead to misunderstandings, frustration, and inefficiency. To manage your workload effectively:

Discuss Priorities: Have an open conversation with your manager about your workload and priorities to ensure alignment of your work hours.

Delegate Smartly: Assign tasks outside your expertise or to those team members who are skilled at resolving the specific issue to optimize productivity and save time.

Learn To Say No: Learn how to politely decline additional tasks when deadlines are tight, unmanageable, and/or inflexible.

Here are some polite phrases that you can use to decline offers or requests effectively while maintaining professionalism and respect.

Phrases for General Refusals:

I appreciate the offer but I'm unable to commit at the moment.

Thank you for considering me but I'll have to pass this time.

Unfortunately, I'm not in a position to take on this additional task right now.

I'm honored by the opportunity but I'll need to decline.

Phrases If You're Overloaded with Work:

I'm currently managing other priorities, so I won't be able to give this task the attention it deserves.

I would love to help, but my current workload won't allow me to contribute effectively.

Phrases That You Can Use as an Alternative:

I can't take this task personally, but I'd be happy to recommend someone who might be a good fit for handling this issue.

I'm unable to assist due to other priorities, but I can offer advice or resources that might help in the completion of your task or project.

Phrases To Use If the Request Doesn't Align with Your Goals:

This seems like a great opportunity, but it's not the right fit for me at this time.

I currently need to prioritize other tasks but thank you for thinking of me.

Phrases To Use If the Person Being Persistent in Assigning the Extra Task:

I have to respectfully decline at the moment but I sincerely appreciate the offer and I wish you success with this project.

Thank you for reaching out to me, but my current work routine doesn't fit the necessary time needed to dedicate to this task.

Break Tasks Down: Divide your larger tasks into smaller, actionable steps to stay focused on your project goal and avoid feeling overwhelmed.

Here are some easy strategies to divide your workload and reap significant results.

Have a Plan: Dividing your tasks requires crucial analysis of the brain and skillset. Avoid carving time between other priorities and set specific one to two hours to plan at the end of your day or week.

Elucidate Roles: For each task assigned to you, you will have a role to play. The key is to leverage your unique strengths and skills to achieve excellence in every role. Focus on specific functions, strengths, and strategies you can apply to complete the task efficiently.

Be Flexible: Even the most functional plans could instantly make you shift priorities. Keep your schedule flexible by creating enough room for any uncalled tasks, events, or delays.

✓ **Lack of Recognition and Appreciation:** It's frustrating when one individual seems to excel in every task, even during unexpected challenges such as power outages. They keep pocketing every compliment that escapes the supervisor, senior, manager, or boss's lips and never allow praise to be directed toward others. This sense of favoritism or exclusion within the team often leaves team members feeling undervalued. The lack of acknowledgment and recognition of others' unconventional contributions leads an individual to the Triple D effect: dissatisfaction, demotivation, and discouragement.

To address these triggering challenges effectively consider making your contributions visible and nurture a collaborative environment:

Adapt During Unexpected Challenges: Immediately notify the IT department about technical difficulties and request assistance to minimize your downtime.

Focus on Alternative Tasks: Plan and work on offline tasks or offline activities that do not rely on technology to stay productive during power outages.

Upskill Yourself: Keep learning essential software or hardware troubleshooting to handling minor technical issues independently, which enhances resourcefulness and makes you an asset to the entire team.

Make Your Work Seen: Update team leads about your progress and contributions to ensure your efforts are visible and acknowledged.

Encourage Team Spirit: Promote

collaboration within teams sharing your skills and supporting colleagues. Valuing each member's contributions builds mutual respect and fosters productive and healthy competition.

✓ **Feedback Criticism:** Handling and delivering criticism, whether constructive or unnecessary, can significantly impact one's productivity and morale. Even constructive feedback could feel like a personal attack if poorly communicated. Effectively handling and delivering criticism is essential for personal and professional growth. Here are some simple steps to manage criticism constructively.

FOUR STEPS TO HANDLE UNNECESSARY CRITICISM

Take a Pause to Analyze: Rather than jumping to a conclusion, take a moment to evaluate the criticism. Is it valid, or is it merely an opinion without substance? People often make negative remarks or judge someone based on their weaknesses and limiting beliefs. Take a moment to analyze the criticism thrown at you and see if it aligns with your behavior or outlook toward the assigned task. You will be surprised to see that half of the criticisms are untrue.

Maintain Professionalism: Avoid responding with anger or defensiveness. Instead, calmly address unwarranted critiques by asking for clarification. Ask

necessary questions to understand the intent behind them and respond selectively.

Set Boundaries: If criticism becomes habitual or unconstructive, address it firmly but respectfully. Assertively communicate the impact of such behavior on your mental well-being. Highlight how unnecessary criticism hinders your productivity towards the project.

Shift Your Focus on Facts: Redirect conversations toward measurable outcomes and facts emphasizing your achievements and valid reasons for your approach. If you constantly receive criticism from a specific supervisor, boss, or colleague, plan and practice your replies beforehand to deliver your point fruitfully.

HOW TO DELIVER CONSTRUCTIVE CRITICISM EFFECTIVELY

Be Specific and Solution-Oriented: Highlight specific areas for improvement and suggest actionable steps, avoiding vague or generalized comments.

Maintain Empathy: Use a respectful tone and frame the feedback as an opportunity for growth rather than a fault-finding mission.

Balance the Feedback: Start with highlighting positive observations to set a constructive tone, address areas of improvement, and conclude your remarks with encouragement.

Focus on Behavior, Not Personality: Address actions or outcomes that could improve the project, not the individual's character, to prevent the feedback from feeling personal.

HOW TO TAKE CONSTRUCTIVE CRITICISM

Adopt a Growth Mindset: Change your perspective toward feedback. Instead of seeing feedback as a flaw highlighter, give yourself a chance to learn and improve rather than taking it as a cruel remark.

Be an Active Listener: Avoid interrupting or jumping to conclusions. Let the critic fully express their thoughts to grasp their core message and respond mindfully.

Clarify and Reflect: Ask questions to ensure you understand the feedback, then reflect on how you can apply it to improve your knowledge.

Thank the Critic: Acknowledge their efforts in sharing insights, even if the delivery wasn't perfect. It's common for people who offer constructive criticism to struggle to form better responses because they care about the receiver's feelings. Expressing gratitude fosters a culture of openness and mutual respect.

When constructive criticism is approached correctly, both in giving and receiving, it could pave the way for enhanced skills, stronger relationships, and greater productivity. By addressing unnecessary criticism firmly and embracing constructive

feedback as a tool for growth, individuals can thrive and transform in every personal and professional challenge.

✓ **Changes in Routines and Procedures:** In a dynamic work environment, especially in IT-driven and software-focused departments, processes and tools are frequently updated to align with the needs of the clients and ensure smooth operations. While these changes aim to improve efficiency and customer satisfaction, they can often trigger feelings of confusion, resistance, and instability among employees.

Here are some simple steps that will help you to navigate such transitions effectively while fostering a positive and productive mindset:

Understand The Reason Behind the Uncalled Change: Seek clarity for the change by engaging with your manager or team leader to understand the rationale. Knowing the purpose can make you less confused and help you stay more connected to the new direction.

Don't Hesitate to Ask Questions: Asking necessary questions clarifies doubts about new processes, software, or policies. The more informed you become, the easier it will be to adapt to a growth mindset.

Keep Yourself Updated: Even when swamped with work, try to set aside a few minutes to educate yourself on topics related to your niche. Familiarize yourself with new tools or procedures through training sessions or self-paced learning.

Staying proactive can help you feel more confident during unplanned transitions.

Share Constructive Feedback: Instead of viewing each change in procedure and routine as a challenge, list opportunities you'll get once you shift to the new process. Share constructive feedback with the team and seniors for improved and refined workflow.

Stay Organized and Flexible: When introduced to a new procedure or work routine, revisit your to-do list and prioritize tasks to align with the updated workflows. Similarly, expect some hiccups while adjusting to the new workflow. Prepare alternative approaches to tackle potential friction.

Work As a Team: Changes often affect multiple departments, so collaboration is key. Share insights, resources, and tips to help each other navigate through the shift.

✓ **Inadequate Resources or Support:** The lack of essential resources, tools, and support from management can create significant roadblocks, leading to frustration, inefficiency, and being undervalued. However, proactively addressing the challenges could transform obstacles into opportunities for improvement and growth.

Here are six steps that you can follow to navigate your stress with inadequate resources or support:

Advocate For What You Need: Clearly outline the resources you require for the completion of the project, how they will contribute to better outcomes, why they are essential for the project, and how the lack of the resources affects your team's overall productivity and project timeline. Use specific data, facts, examples, or comparisons to solidify and strengthen your request for client satisfaction.

Leverage Internal Networks: Reach out to colleagues, teams, or other departments to know if they have exclusive access to the tools and expertise you require. Promote collaboration within teams for a creative workaround and share knowledge and resources to bridge the gap effectively.

Explore Alternative Solutions: Look out for external sources or keep your knowledge updated on alternative software, templates, or online courses that could ease the tension of completing a project with limited tools. Researching free affordable tools could also help inspire out-of-the-box thinking and creative problem-solving.

Communicate Challenges: Keep authorities informed of the challenges your team faces due to limited resources. Frame discussions around solutions rather than complaining about problems to maintain a constructive tone and avoid being seen as resistant to short-term or long-term challenges. This also further reinforces the urgency of addressing the issue and showcases your commitment to finding solutions.

Focus on High-Impact Tasks: Focus on tasks that will greatly impact the project's completion before shifting your focus to supplementary duties. Taking this approach will maximize your team's efficiency and optimize outcomes.

Propose Long-term Investments: If inadequate resources are a constant battle for every project your team is being assigned, suggest the higher authorities invest in resources that resolve immediate issues to enhance long-term productivity and employee satisfaction. Track how new resources optimize your team's growth and progress to document outcomes for future support.

When faced with inadequate resources, proactive communication, strategic planning, and creative problem-solving are key to resolving issues promptly. By advocating for support, fostering collaboration, and leveraging alternatives, you can easily switch resource limitations into an opportunity to demonstrate resilience and innovation while driving your projects forward.

✓ **Challenges in Work-Life Balance:** Struggling to balance personal life with work commitments is a common challenge faced by every working individual. This imbalance can lead to unnecessary stress, guilt, and reduced well-being. Maintaining a healthy work-life balance is not just about managing time effectively but also about prioritizing your overall well-being.

A few simple steps that you can nurture to create a balance and enjoy the best of both worlds are:

Define Work Hours: Create a structured schedule with dedicated work hours and stick to it.

Limit Multitasking: Rather than focusing on multiple projects, divide a time slot for each process and avoid blending work and personal tasks as it dilutes your focus and creates more stress.

Disconnect After Work: Turn off notifications and avoid checking emails or messages outside work hours unless it is non-negotiable. However, do not overdo it, even if it is non-negotiable.

Communicate Clear Boundaries: Inform and update your colleagues and supervisors about your availability and personal commitments. Communicate your work boundaries and specify how much advance notice they need for you to address urgent work matters effectively.

Prioritize Breaks: Unplug regularly by taking short breaks during work hours and schedule self-care practices like spending time with your family and friends outside work. Don't delve into topics related to work. Indulge your mind in lighthearted activities, like games, shopping, vacations, meditation, exercise, and hobbies. Switching off from thoughts regarding work helps your mind rejuvenate and increases concentration.

Be Present: Work-related thoughts can be persistent, intruding on personal time. To refocus on the task, pause when you catch your mind wandering. Take a deep breath and consciously shift your focus and attention to the present moment and surroundings.

Always remember, work-life balance is not about perfecting your schedule but alignment. This simple realization will ultimately lead you to greater satisfaction and success in both areas of your life.

Actionable Takeaway

a. Be assertive in your responses without compromising your needs.

b. The key to resolving any conflict is regulating the temperature gauge to warm. Cool down hot conflicts and warm up cold conflicts. Warm conflicts are progressive and productive.

c. While interacting, identify and recognize patterns to understand your initial emotional triggers to navigate challenging situations efficiently.

Quick Win:

Clear Boundaries and open communication are the foundation of a healthy work relationship.

CHAPTER 2: THE PSYCHOLOGY BEHIND OUTSMARTING MANIPULATORS

Manipulation is one of the tactics used in dark psychology, involving dishonest and harmful social influence, often at the expense of abusing someone's emotions and well-being. It plays a significant yet insidious role in social dynamics, involving actions, behaviors, and words intended to influence or control another person's thoughts, behaviors, and reactions.

Humans have an inherent ability to be manipulative or deceptive, but the main difference lies in an individual's personality traits or mental health conditions. It typically involves underhanded tactics such as seduction, suggestion, coercion, and blackmail.

Manipulation differs from persuasion and influence as it involves exploiting the emotional vulnerabilities of others for personal gain, making it coercive and harmful. Influence and persuasion are seen as positive or neutral activities that involve a genuine intent to guide or change negative thoughts, patterns, and behaviors without violating a person's autonomy, whereas manipulation is inherently negative.

COMMON ELEMENTS OF MANIPULATION IN A WORKPLACE

Below are some common elements of manipulation and phrases preferred by manipulators that you may often encounter in a workplace:

GASLIGHTING

Gaslighting is when someone causes another person to doubt their reality, perceptions, and sanity. In the workplace, this can occur among colleagues and managers who deny something they said or did, suggesting that the person is imagining things or being overly sensitive.

For example, when someone says, *"Are you sure you remember it that way? I don't recall it like that,"* even though they know the speaker is being truthful.

Such words and actions create confusion and self-doubt in the targeted individual's mind. Over time, the targeted individual may feel anxious, lose confidence, or question their own judgment, even over trivial matters.

This practice is potentially damaging as it erodes trust, creates a toxic environment, and makes the manipulated individual feel invalidated and insecure.

GUILT TRIPPING

Guilt-tripping occurs when someone makes another person feel guilty for their right actions, positive thoughts, and good decisions in order to get them to comply with negative demands or expectations. In a workplace setting, this can involve a supervisor, manager, boss, or coworker constantly reminding you of their unneeded favors and how much they have done for you or how many sacrifices they have made pushing you to feel obligated to help them out.

Phrases like, *"I can't believe you would do this to me after I've always helped you out,"* are often used by manipulators for guilt-tripping. This psychological tactic leverages a person's compassion and sense of responsibility, causing them to feel guilty and pressured, even over trivial matters. This often leads to an unhealthy cycle of compliance and resentment.

PASSIVE AGGRESSION

Passive aggression is an indirect way of expressing negative feelings rather than addressing them directly or honestly. In a work setting, this behavior manifests through sarcasm, backhanded compliments, procrastination, or the intentional inefficiency of a manipulator.

An example of passive aggression might be, *"Fine, I'll just do it myself since no one else seems capable."* This type of sentence or behavior often creates confusion and tension between team members and colleagues, as the manipulator intentionally avoids open communication and confrontation.

The targeted individuals feel guilty and frustrated as they get stuck in a constant loop of reading between the lines, which further damages team morale, fosters misunderstandings, and breeds unproductivity.

WITHHOLDING INFORMATION

Withholding information means keeping or intentionally hiding crucial details or resources to maintain control over a team or individual. This type of manipulation controls the flow of information and holds power over a situation, team, or person.

In a work setting, you might hear a supervisor, manager, or boss say, *"Oh, I thought I told you about that, but I guess I forgot,"* when it becomes inconvenient for them to hide or withhold information that could help the team or individual perform better or make informed decisions.

This psychological trick often leads to poor decision-making, uncalled frustration, and a sense of unfair treatment. It impacts the overall work timeline, causing project delays or failures.

BLAME SHIFTING

Blame shifting is the act of making others take responsibility for one's mistakes or failures. In the workplace, it often involves a manager or coworker blaming an individual or a team for a responsibility that is completely out of their control or is a collective mistake of team members and seniors.

For example, if someone comments, *'It's your fault the project failed; you didn't follow through as promised,'* or *'It was your idea that led to the team's failure,'* this deflects accountability and places unnecessary pressure on the person blamed or held accountable.

This tactic fosters a sense of victimization and creates a culture of fear where team members or employees are afraid to take risks, express innovative ideas, or speak up, fearing they might be wrongfully blamed and held accountable for decisions, mistakes, situations, and outcomes that are not theirs to bear.

FAVORITISM

Favoritism is the act of showing preferential treatment or being biased toward certain employees, which creates division and dependence. This can be showcased as giving better opportunities, more support, and leverage to individuals who can easily be overpowered by other team members who are truly deserving of the facilities.

For instance, a supervisor or manager might say, *'You know I trust that employee with this task to complete it efficiently,'* even though it is a task that could easily deliver better results or outcomes. This kind of bias creates division among team members, makes workplaces hostile, undermines morale, discourages teamwork, and leads to feelings of unfairness among employees who feel undervalued or overlooked. It can damage a team's cohesion and hinder productivity.

EMOTIONAL EXPLOITATION

Emotional exploitation is when someone takes advantage of your vulnerability and feelings. You often might have a hard time denying sincere requests or helping people who are in need. Manipulators take advantage of these kinds of emotions, forcing and pushing an individual to a certain extent that they get involved in activities, projects, and expectations that solely benefit the manipulator.

This tactic is exercised by playing on someone's emotions, such as guilt, empathy, or sympathy, to get them to act in the manipulator's favor. Phrases like, *"I have such a hard time at home; I need this support from you right now"* are used to create an emotional obligation for the target to assist or overlook their own needs. Over time this kind of emotional exploitation leads to burnout as the targeted individual is always focused on making the manipulator's demands met forgetting about their own well-being.

UNDERMINING CONFIDENCE

This psychological tactic involves unnecessary criticism using actions or words that make a person feel inadequate or doubt their abilities. It is used to weaken an individual sense of self and increase their dependence on the manipulators.

In the workplace, this can look like comments such as, *"Are you sure, you are qualified for this? I have seen others do it better."* When a person's confidence is continually challenged, they start to question their skills, doubt their decisions, hesitate to take on new challenges, or withdraw from contributing innovative ideas. This further gives rise to situations that not only affect

the individual's performance but can also create a discouraging environment that stifles creativity and collaboration.

OVERLOADING WITH WORK

In the workplace, overloading employees with work often manifests in situations where a manager assigns an absurd amount of work to an individual and uses phrases like, *'I need these tasks done by the end of the day. I know, it's a lot, but I'm counting on you.'*

On the surface level, this may seem like the manager is requesting to prioritize the tasks as they trust the individual but over time assigning excessive tasks with unreasonable deadlines with the expectation that the person will comply without complaint, pressures the employee into prioritizing futile requests over their workload and well-being. This tactic also leads to increased amounts of mistakes, exhaustion, and a feeling of being trapped, causing the employee to be more pliable and less likely to assert the boundaries.

USING FLATTERY

Manipulators use flattery to create a sense of indebtedness or obligation. For example, a colleague or supervisor might say, *"You are the only one who can do this task correctly. Everyone else falls short when I consider your skills and talent."*

While compliments can be sincere and genuine, manipulators use this tactic to create a sense of specialness in the targeted individual's mind, which can be leveraged later to get them to agree to requests and expectations. It also creates a sense of being seen and valued, which makes the target more vulnerable to exploitation as they try to maintain that perceived pseudo-positive impression.

THREATS AND INTIMIDATION

In the workplace, threats and intimidation could range from subtle hints of retribution to explicit threats about job security or performance. For example, threatening an individual or employee using phrases like *"If you don't meet this deadline, there could be serious consequences,"* puts unnecessary pressure on an individual to deliver results without fail. It further affects the individual's productivity and creativity required to perform optimally.

This psychological tactic, which uses fear or the implication of negative consequences to force someone into compliance, creates an atmosphere of fear and resentment, leading individuals to avoid speaking up about potential issues, limited resource struggles, sharing ideas, feeling anxious, or resisting unreasonable demands. This, in turn, can lead to mental health issues and cause serious harm to the well-being of the targeted person.

CREATING DEPENDENCY

This psychological scheme is used by making the individual feel and believe that they cannot succeed without the manipulator's involvement. The manipulator might use words or sentences like, *"I will handle this project, but only because I know you will struggle with it."*

Phrases like this reinforce the idea that the individual is incapable of making necessary decisions and doubts their abilities. They often feel that they cannot achieve significant results and success without the manipulator's input. This further solidifies the manipulator's power and control to govern the individual's work life and decisions.

SELECTIVE TRUTHS

Selective Truths are spoken by manipulators to hide their real agenda. For instance, a senior, supervisor, or manager might say *"The meeting went great, everyone was impressed with the work."* while hiding details that they took the entire credit of all the team members during the presentation. This method distorts the perception of reality and can lead to misinformed decisions or confusion. It influences people's views and opinions over critical situations making it difficult to assess the full picture or act appropriately.

EMOTIONAL BLACKMAIL

In the workplace, emotional blackmail may sound like, *"If you don't do this for me, I will have no choice but to pull my support from your project."* This creates a sense of fear, guilt, and emotional obligation to make the targeted individual comply as failing will lead to negative consequences.

Emotional Blackmail is an abusive technique that creates a hostile work environment and fosters an atmosphere where employees are forced to choose between their values and their job security.

ISOLATING COLLEAGUES

This psychological strategy is used by manipulators to spark a sense of complete dependency among targeted individuals and reinforces the idea that the manipulator is the sole source of understanding and support.

Sentences like, *"I'm the only one who understands what you are dealing with. You can't talk to anyone else about this"* are often used even if the manipulator themselves tries to create circumstances that cut the support off from the individual or input of their peers.

Gradually, this isolates the individual from the entire team leaving them more susceptible to further manipulation and preventing them from seeking external help or advice.

Manipulative tactics can leave lasting damage, impacting an individual's self-esteem, emotional health, and overall well-being. Recognizing and understanding the roots of manipulative behaviors is the key to protecting yourself from difficult people who exploit emotions.

HOW DIFFICULT PEOPLE EXPLOIT EMOTIONS

Imagine this: You've finally secured your first job at a marketing firm, where everyone operates under tight deadlines. With a heart of gold, you decide to showcase your genuine nature and help people in need whenever you have extra time. After a few projects helping team members and completing your tasks efficiently, you encounter a colleague with an unassuming demeanor, always quick to smile and share tales of her hardships. You start admiring her openness and how she doesn't shy away from talking about her struggles—her health, her family's financial woes, and the endless challenges life throws at her.

One afternoon, as you rushed to meet a deadline, the colleague approached your desk with a trembling voice. You notice that her face is masked with stress, so you ask if everything's okay. She replies, *"I've had a terrible week with everything going on in my family. I hate to ask, but could you help me finish this report?"*

Her eyes welled up, and your heart sank. How could you say no after learning about every minute of her struggles and each hardship she'd gone through? So, you decide to help. For weeks, it becomes a pattern. Her stories became more intense, and her requests more frequent. She would often sigh or use phrases like *"I'm relieved that I don't have to put up a happy mask around you at least"* or during team meetings, she often hinted at you about her struggles to ensure your attention and sympathy were firmly on her.

Every time she approached you with a new request, you found it difficult to deny, sacrificing your evenings and your weekends to support her. She praised you for your unwavering support, asking you to believe that you were making a real difference in her life.

One day, while chatting with a colleague, you discover something shocking about her. The stories she shared with you had never been shared with anyone else. She always behaved cheerful and unburdened while interacting with others. That's when it hits you: the manipulative colleague has been continuously leveraging your empathy to ease her workload and avoid responsibility.

Consequence: You sacrificed and jeopardized your well-being and mental peace to help a person who was manipulating you with her victim mentality.

WHAT DO WE MEAN WHEN WE SAY VICTIM MENTALITY?

The victim mentality is a powerful manipulation tool in which an individual constantly portrays themselves as the wronged party, regardless of the situation. This, in turn, shifts the targeted individual's attention and sympathy toward the manipulator while deflecting accountability.

Manipulators who play the victim card often craft elaborate narratives about their hardships and mistreatment. They strategically weave stories that contain a perfect balance of truth and lies, designed to evoke sympathy and distract targeted individuals from their own shortcomings or harmful behaviors. It helps them gain an advantage in interpersonal dynamics, as people are less likely to challenge or criticize someone they perceive as vulnerable and oppressed.

HOW PLAYING THE VICTIM CARD WORKS

Empathetic individuals often have a heightened sensitivity towards guilt, as they deeply value the well-being of others. They find it difficult to turn a blind eye to situations in which they know they could help with just a little extra effort. The key word is "extra." Manipulators exploit this trait by portraying themselves as someone who needs constant care, attention, and support, making you feel compelled to intervene and stand up for them.

For example, a manipulative coworker might frequently remind you of how they were overlooked in their previous roles, how their remarks are always dismissed by their seniors or colleagues, or use exaggerated narratives with elements of truth to gain undue sympathy and avoid accountability for their poor performance. This puts the targeted individual in a vulnerable position, where they are compelled to feel emotionally invested. This dynamic further drains the individual as they are continuously drawn into the manipulator's fabricated issues.

THE AFTER EFFECTS OF EMPATHY EXPLOITATION

When empathetic individuals are manipulated, they often invest significant emotional energy into supporting the manipulator which leads to burnout or emotional exhaustion. Similarly, manipulators often undermine their targets' confidence by making them feel responsible for the manipulator's well-being. This can lead to feelings of inadequacy and self-doubt in the targeted individual, often internalizing the manipulator's criticisms or unmet demands. Over time, the empathetic individual may feel trapped, undervalued, or resentful, while the manipulator continues to take advantage of their kindness.

HOW TO PROTECT YOURSELF FROM EMPATHY EXPLOITATION

Manipulators often target individuals with a strong sense of empathy and compassion. For manipulators, these noble attributes are perceived as a tool for exploitation rather than a powerful and sensible trait. They often target individuals who are gullible and emotional, effortlessly blurring the lines between genuine need and calculated deceit, which further leaves the individual feeling drained, guilty, and confused.

To protect yourself from being seen as vulnerable, from becoming a target of empathy exploitation, or from falling prey to the hands of a manipulator, you must learn the art of reading and understanding the body language of a manipulator. You need to refine your skills in recognizing patterns, behaviors, and tactics. Setting healthy boundaries and learning to balance kindness with self-preservation is the key to safeguarding your emotional well-being without compromising your capacity or quality of care.

Here are the five methods that you can implement in your daily life and work life to avoid being manipulated:

Recognizing Red Flags:

Stay alert to behaviors that signal potential manipulation such as:

- Excessive Victim Narratives.

- Patterns of Deflecting Responsibility.

- Frequent Guilt Tripping and Emotional Appeals.

- Lack of Reciprocation in Discussions and Conflicts.

Setting Pre-Boundaries:

When you are empathetic, saying 'no' often becomes the most difficult task compared to other work activities. Empathetic individuals often fall into the endless web of self-criticism when they straight-up deny a request, even if it is highly negotiable. The best way to steer clear of unreasonable demands and requests is by setting pre-boundaries. Practice assertive communication using phrases like;

- *I understand you are going through a tough time, but currently, I'm not well-equipped or able to take on this responsibility.*

- *I care about you but I also need to focus on my priorities.*

Be bold and unpredictable when dealing with manipulators, as it often confuses them and makes them question their limited perspective of you.

Encouraging Accountability:

Instead of stepping in as their rescuer, encourage manipulators to take responsibility for their own actions. Use firm and clear responses such as:

I feel sorry to hear that, but what steps or approaches are you thinking of taking to address this issue?

I can support you in your decisions, but I would not be able to fix it for you.

Prioritize Self Care:

Sometimes manipulators are disguised as the person you need to assist or address your work progress, such as a senior coordinator, team leader, supervisor, senior colleague, manager, or boss.

In such situations, prioritize self-care to prevent emotional exhaustion. Spend time in activities that make you feel recharged and help you stay focused on your task.

Seek External Support:

If you find it difficult to avoid a manipulator, call out their toxic behavior. Consult a trusted friend, mentor, or higher authorities and voice out the negative patterns and tactics you are being victimized. Develop strategies to address them effectively and switch jobs or departments if possible.

There are also other hidden motives for which manipulators take leverage over our noble traits. In the next chapter, we will discuss essential elements to identify the real motives of manipulators and how to tackle each one of them.

ESSENTIAL ELEMENTS TO IDENTIFY HIDDEN MOTIVES

Hidden motives are concealed intentions that drive people to act in ways that often seem misleading or deceptive. These motives usually stem from the four basic motives of behavior: fear, personal incentives, guilt, or selfish desires. These ulterior motives are often considered sneaky and self-serving, focusing on dominating and exercising control over others for achievement, growth, and affiliation. However, it is not always malicious and depends entirely on the individual, as some people use it to safeguard themselves from threatening pitfalls.

Fear: Acting out of insecurity or self-preservation.

Incentive: Driven by personal gain, such as financial benefit or career advancement.

Guilt: Using others' emotions to avoid accountability.

Selfishness: Seeking power, recognition, or control.

These are the four foundational drivers that help an individual detect whether someone's actions align with their stated intentions.

SIGNS OF HIDDEN MOTIVES

The best way to spot someone's hidden motives is by observing and understanding how they make you feel. Gut feelings or intuition are great tools for identifying the concealed intentions behind someone's words or actions. Negative emotions such as feeling controlled, confused, or upset after dealing with someone who leaves you anxious for a while are true signs that the person is lying to your face.

Let's explore five easy ways to spot hidden motives and actionable strategies to stop

being undermined by manipulators and narcissists.

1. Inconsistent Behavior

When was the last time you noticed unusual body language during an interaction? Subtle physical cues often reveal more than words ever do, especially when someone is hiding their true intentions. Signs such as forced eye contact signal that the manipulator is trying to appear trustworthy and wants you to believe their fabricated lies.

When a person lies, they try to mimic the natural body language they use when speaking the truth. Their way of maintaining eye contact often feels like they are staring at you to notice if you are being convinced by their lie.

Fidgeting and excessive blinking are other common signs, as liars often struggle to maintain composure, signaling their inner conflict between fabricating a believable story and maintaining a facade.

Pay close attention to their actions, as they often contradict their words.

For Example, a colleague or supervisor who often praises teamwork but secretly withholds key information, such as taking all the credit for the teamwork during the board meeting.

Hidden Element: Micro-expressions—quick, involuntary facial expressions or behaviors used to hide their fear of being caught or to mirror your gestures in an attempt to appear trustworthy and relatable.

2. Unexplained Changes in Priorities and Over-Justification

Sudden shifts in attitude and plans without proper notice are an attempt to hide or conceal real intentions.

When assigned a task to complete while collaborating with a teammate, it's important to be transparent about your skills, plans, and progress to tackle the project effectively. When a teammate tries to be manipulative or hide their secret agenda, they will often use phrases like *"I thought you already knew about the update"* or provide excessive or irrelevant explanations for simple actions.

For Example, A person repeatedly emphasizes a minor point to steer your attention away from the truth. This tactic is often referred to as the 'lie arc' where a person tries to overwhelm the listener with unnecessary details, making the truth harder to discern.

Hidden Element: Subtly blaming others for delays or confusion to deflect responsibilities by avoiding specific details about timelines or outcomes, making it harder to hold accountable.

3. Emotional Manipulation

Conversations with manipulators are rarely focused on finding a mutual solution. Their main motive is to convince you for their benefit, often fixating on one goal and steering the conversation toward an endpoint that serves their hidden agenda.

Emotions like guilt, fear, empathy, and sympathy are traits manipulators use as effective tools to gain leverage and control the words and actions of their targets.

For Example, a work friend may make you feel guilty for declining their unreasonable requests with phrases like *"I couldn't believe you would do that to me,"* even though you had other important tasks to prioritize.

Hidden Element: Sharing half-truths or intentionally misunderstanding your point to hold you accountable for their mistakes.

4. Self-Centered Conversations

Manipulators and narcissists often feign genuine interest in others, using their targets to meet their own needs. They may pretend to listen attentively, beginning the conversation by asking about your thoughts, opinions, or feelings, but often shift the topic to their achievements, struggles, or well-being.

It often becomes evident during conversations that their focus is on portraying themselves as the victim of all wrongdoings. They often shift blame to external circumstances or others to gain sympathy and make themselves appear unthreatening.

For instance, when you share a personal challenge, they may console you with phrases like *"I can relate to you, but I've been through worse."* In their mind, it's always a competition to appear stronger, better, or more vulnerable. They feel threatened when they can't get the attention they want, so they often use exaggerated stories to seek validation or admiration for their efforts and sacrifices.

Over time, their monopolization of conversations leaves the target emotionally drained, fostering feelings of frustration and neglect. It also undermines mutual respect in relationships and compels the target to question their thoughts, beliefs, and worth.

Hidden Element: Cutting you off mid-sentence to direct the focus to their struggles, always making your experiences seem insignificant compared to their exaggerated truths.

5. Power Plays

Power plays are often used by higher authorities, such as a supervisor, manager, or team leader. People who manipulate others for their benefit often use twisted strategies to assert dominance and gain control over them.

For example, a manager might assign you an excessive amount of work with unreasonable deadlines. When you voice your concerns or struggles to find common ground, they may say things like, *"I know it's a lot, but if you fail to submit the project by the deadline, I'll be forced to pull my support from your team."*

The main purpose of using these subtle power plays is to keep the target threatened and make them believe they won't be able to outshine the manipulator or make progress without their support.

Hidden Element: Offering minor concessions to appear supportive, only to leverage them later and make you feel indebted, or justify unreasonable demands using vague references to higher-ups or company policies to assert their dominance over you.

Now that you know the hidden elements of how manipulators and narcissists hide their true agenda. Let's learn how to safeguard ourselves, take control of such interactions, and distance ourselves from toxic work dynamics.

HOW TO PROTECT YOURSELF FROM PEOPLE WITH HIDDEN MOTIVES

Manipulators are like illusionists; they charm, disarm, and, before you know it, catch you in their web. They are skilled at making subtle gestures. Instead of bold moves, they operate through whispers, kind affirmations, and pseudo-favors that seem helpful and harmless. The key word is "seem."

They put you in situations that highlight their generosity and perceived transparency, making you question your own decisions. But beneath their veneer of generosity lies an intricate game of control.

To guard yourself against the hidden motives of manipulators, focus on honing your ability to recognize their tactics and cultivate a shield of oblivion, confidence, wit, and discernment.

Given below are nine psychological safety measures that you could implement to fight back against a manipulator.

Return All Favors: Manipulators thrive by making their target comply with unwanted favors. If a person at work is excessively sweet toward you—such as bringing you a cup of coffee even when you didn't ask for it, fixing a minor mistake or issue even when it's negotiable, cloaking flattery as a compliment, portraying you as their savior for every trivial difficulty, sharing selective confidential information to show they rely on and trust you, over-empathizing with your struggles, or volunteering to help with a task you don't need support for—these are all common tactics.

These are some common practices of a manipulator, which can be termed pseudo-favors. When a person doesn't have a hidden motive to manipulate you, they rarely keep track of favors or unsolicited gestures they do for you. You'll often find yourself reminding them that they helped and saved you when you were in desperate need.

But people with hidden motives act differently. They highlight every small gesture they make to help you and expect you to comply. They make it difficult for you to forget or overlook their contributions to your work life and projects, so they can later leverage those actions to ask for unreasonable favors you would be reluctant to agree to.

One effective technique to steer clear of a manipulator's needless benevolence is by returning every favor. If a manipulator offers you a cup of coffee, politely decline with a phrase like, *"Thank you for bringing this, but I'd appreciate it if you could ask me first before buying it in the future."* When the opportunity arises, return the favor by buying them something equivalent, using a phrase like, *"Since you bought me a cup of coffee last time, I thought you might enjoy this new drink."*

Phrases like these are effective in avoiding unnecessary demands, as they keep the scorecard neutral without one party overcompensating the other. If you ignore these small favors, they will eventually manifest into bigger risks, like jeopardizing your work schedule to complete uncredited tasks for the manipulator.

Asks Irrelevant Counter Questions: One thing manipulators least expect is someone quick enough to stand up to their deceptive tricks. If a person with hidden motives asks for your opinion on irrelevant or unnecessary tasks, question them back or use sharp, witty replies.

For example, when someone asks, *"Could you help me finish this project?"* even though they know you need to prioritize other tasks, respond by asking, *"Could you help me finish my shift tomorrow?"* or, *"Would you be able to help me finish these X tasks by the end of the day?"*

If the person agrees, make sure to assign them tasks equal to or double the amount they are asking you to complete. This psychological trick disinterests the manipulator in deceiving you and fosters the idea in their mind that they are the one complying with your needs.

Here are some general phrases you can use to divert the attention of the manipulator or portray yourself as a tough target:

a. *Do you expect me to do this? You know, this is not in my best interest.*

b. *Do you care about my opinion? I think you're trying to act sly for your own benefit.*

c. *Do you think you could support my decision, even if it doesn't benefit you at all?*

d. *I would never be able to reciprocate the favors you're offering. Are you sure you'd still like to help or contribute to this project?*

e. *Are you sure this is the last favor you're asking of me this month? I think you've used that excuse quite a few times before to get me to comply with your requests.*

These types of rhetorical questions put the manipulator off guard as they begin contradicting their own words to hide their real agenda. Over time, this will plant a seed in their head that you are a difficult target to dupe.

Highlight Their Names: Our names are an integral part of our identity. They represent who we are and how we want the world to recognize us. It defines us as our personal brand and whether in praise or criticism; hearing our names called by a different person often creates a deep emotional response that resonates with our sense of self.

Skilled communicators and, often, manipulators leverage this to establish a connection that leaves a lasting impression on our subconscious mind. This is a timeless tactic often used by great leaders, politicians, and even peers to influence an individual's mind and make them believe in their way of thinking and speaking. However, unlike great leaders and politicians who work for a better cause by shaping our perspective toward abundance and growth, manipulators exploit it to create a sense of false endearment, friendliness, and trust in the targeted individual.

Incorporating someone's preferred name into a conversation is an effective strategy to make them feel valued, seen, heard, and understood. It enhances communication, builds rapport with the other party, and makes interactions warmer.

Interestingly, this also serves as an effective tool to catch manipulators off guard, as they often perceive you as threatening rather than weak. If someone calls out your name for a non-preferred project or activity and says, for example, *"Susan, I never thought you would do this to me"* or *"Ken, I couldn't think I would be able to replace your skills for this task"*, know that they are trying to convince you to take up that un-credited project or foster a sense of guilt so that you start blaming yourself for their shortcomings.

Respond thoughtfully by using the form of the name they prefer to create an impression of awareness and counteract the situation. This technique of using their name in your replies potentially discourages their manipulative behavior. For example, let's say the above phrases are used by a manipulator named Jennie. Earlier, you noticed her correcting a colleague or a supervisor to call her Jen instead of her full name as she prefers the shorter version of her name.

So, if you need to deny Jennie the manipulator's request, you would say, *'Jen, I'm really sorry to hear how you're feeling. Have you considered trying the task yourself, or perhaps reaching out to someone else for help?"* Offer constructive alternatives as you deny their request, forcing the manipulator to look for an alternative solution.

Don't Forget to Play the Stare Game:

Eye contact is a powerful tool for asserting dominance and control over others. It's an unspoken form of communication humans use to convey their strength. Just like in the animal kingdom, it conveys power, authority, and supremacy over other beings; humans are no different. When someone stares at us with an intense gaze, we feel uneasy and uncomfortable, which makes us instinctively look away.

Manipulative individuals, or people with hidden motives, often use it as a weapon when they need to assert control and dominance over their target. But you can easily turn the tables by firmly denying their request and playing the stare game.

Here's how you can win over a manipulator by maintaining steady eye contact and playing the stare game.

When the manipulator or anyone with hidden motives approaches you with an unwanted offer, favor, or advice, shift your stance toward them and take a moment before firmly denying the request. Maintain a steady gaze with a calm demeanor to reinforce your boundaries without escalating the situation.

If the person is a skilled manipulator, chances are they'll intensify their gaze to assert dominance and control over you. Instead of getting terrified and avoiding their gaze, speak up about your priorities and let them know they're making you uncomfortable.

By using their tactic against them, you can make them lose focus, feel unsettled, and make yourself appear as someone resolute in your decision.

Make Them Count Your Favors: This psychological strategy works best for manipulators or people who often generalize your favors. Maybe in the past, you agreed to complete one or two tasks to showcase teamwork, and since then, they've assumed you'll comply with every unwelcome task assigned to you.

For example, let's say you previously assisted a colleague, Alex, by fixing a major mistake in the task assigned to him for your group project, which eventually led you to cover some of his late-night shifts due to an emergency at his home. Recognizing your willingness to help, Alex sincerely thanked you and soon after, he started piling up more last-minute tasks to you.

He often approached you to swap shifts with him, fix errors in his submitted project, back him up for his absence in team meetings, and cover a missed deadline, without considering your pending tasks, risks, or schedule.

When you try to decline his requests, he generalizes your willingness to help by saying, *'But you've always helped me out before. I thought I could count on you.'* or highlight instances where he's reciprocated your favors with small acts of pretending kindness, like holding the elevator door for you when you ran late, bringing you a cup of your favorite coffee blend when you were buried in work, and flattering you for your unmatched skills and expertise.

This is a classic manipulation strategy where the manipulator takes isolated incidents, often out of context, and presents them as recurring patterns of your behavior and personality. Even if you agreed to lend a helping hand once due to unforeseen circumstances, they'll fuel you with guilt and turn that one scenario into an unspoken obligation to comply with every absurd request they make.

To address such an exploiter, you need to challenge their generalization of your favors and prompt the manipulator to specify instances supporting their claim. Interrogate them to provide specific examples. For instance; you could respond to them by asking, *'Alex, I understand you feel I've always helped you to cover your shifts and have been safeguarding you against your shortcomings, but could you please help me recall and list all the favors in which I willingly helped you?'*

This question puts the burden of proof on the manipulator and helps you assert control over their false narrative. It compels the manipulator to confront the reality of a situation and reveals the exaggeration in their attempt to generalize your kindness.

Repeat To Reinforce: This strategy is a fun game you can play to win against a manipulator. Nobody likes to hear a broken record, especially if it's playing a song they hate. Manipulative individuals detest hearing phrases that don't align with their needs.

If you're having trouble drawing boundaries with the manipulative individual, create a universal response and repeat it until the manipulator gets tired of bombarding you with their troublesome requests. For example, let's say there's a colleague who always complains that you never heed her requests and always misunderstand her. She might hold you accountable by saying;

She: You never pay attention to what I have to say.

You: I'm sorry you feel that way.

She: What's the point of being sorry, you will misunderstand me again.

You: Well, it's human to misunderstand. I don't see any harm in you explaining it to me again.

She: But that's just wasting time on a single task.

You: Why don't you invest that energy into completing the task yourself?

She: But I'm struggling to complete it.

You: Have you tried reaching out for external resources?

She: There are no potential resources that could help me to complete this project.

You: Then, what makes you think I could help you with your task?

She: You are excellent at this specific task.

You: Well, thank you for acknowledging my expertise. But if I had to complete it, I'd use that X resource. Why don't you invest your time doing the same?

She: But then, I'd need more time, and currently, the entire team is on a time crunch.

You: You can always reach out to our manager with your request.

She: But I'm not on good terms with our manager. You know that.

You: Great, then you can use this opportunity to show how sincere you are about completing your task.

She: No, that would just get me into more trouble.

You: How would asking for genuine help get you into more trouble?

She: Leave. You never understand and help me out.

You: I'm sorry you feel that way.

She: What's the point of saying sorry? You're not understanding the simple fact that I need your help to complete this project.

You: It's human to misunderstand. Besides, I don't see any need to help you with your task. You're well-equipped to complete it yourself.

She: I can't do it by myself. I've tried my best.

You: Why don't you explain again the steps you took while trying to finish this project?

She: I don't see the point in explaining it to you. You still won't understand.

You: I'm sorry you feel that way.

Make sure you interact with these phrases in a monotone voice. Stripping your voice out of every emotion to not reciprocate with the manipulator's anxiety will further frustrate them to continue the conversation with you. Over time, they would get disinterested in targeting you for their manipulation as they will build a perspective of receiving the same responses again and again.

Be Oblivious: Our instinct is to react or act defensively, especially when our values, beliefs, and self-perception feel threatened. Manipulators exploit this defensive instinct by twisting their responses, gaslighting us, or steering the interaction to align with their agenda.

Imagine this: you and the manipulator are in a silent disco, and you see the manipulator trying to sync their lips with the song playing in both of your headsets. But they have no idea that you never actually turned up the volume on your headset. You simply observe the manipulator struggling to match their gestures and lip-sync with the lyrics they are hearing. Once they get tired and wait for you to sing the next verse, you simply smile because you have no idea what song they're asking you to sing along with.

When they probe for your attention, you simply respond with concrete words or short sentences such as: *'Interesting,' 'Is that so?'* or *'Hmm.'*

Keep yourself occupied with another task while you deal with the manipulator in this situation. This will keep 90% of your focus on the task, rather than solely concentrating on the manipulator's words. If they ask you to shift your attention to them, tell them you have other tasks to prioritize later. Now is the only time in your schedule to complete this task.

Whenever you catch yourself drifting from your work and focusing more on the manipulator's words, redirect your mind to your current progress on the task. When the manipulator approaches you, never make yourself completely available. If they trap you during lunch hour, steer clear of the conversation using phrases like: *'I'd prefer not to discuss work during breaks. It hampers my productivity.'* or *'Would you mind if I connect with my friends or family during lunch? I hardly get time to talk to my parents.'*

Manipulators rarely approach you when a third party is involved, as it makes them feel threatened that the third perspective might reveal their deceptive nature.

Create an Exclusive Personal Boundary: Never mix professional affairs with personal issues. Similarly, never give a manipulator the same professional space where other team members can discuss their genuine needs. Create an exclusive personal boundary for the manipulative individual and get them to believe that it is for their benefit.

For example, if an individual often approaches you in person to ask for uncredited favors, ask them to text you instead. Don't view the messages if the favors are too frequent. When they ask for an explanation, just say, *'I was caught up in other tasks, so I didn't check for any updates.'* Some software and communication platforms are also equipped with features that help you view messages without the notification of being seen or read. Use them to your advantage.

Manipulators love intruding into personal spaces and try to stay close to learn more about their weaknesses. Make sure to never share the same professional space with the manipulator where you mostly address your team's genuine issues. This will further help you to have solid proof against the manipulator's future tactics.

Learn to Love Yourself: Manipulators thrive by highlighting our flaws and making us feel guilty for having them. No individual on this earth or beyond is perfect. Perfection itself is subjective. So, stop ruining your beauty sleep over the remarks of someone who has no clue about the struggles you've gone through to secure the job. Whenever a manipulator charges you with an absurd ideology or a flaw, don't react or try to justify your perspective. Instead, take a moment to analyze whether it's an issue worth investing your time and energy in clarifying.

Most of the time, you can spot the exaggeration in their words, allowing you to dismiss it with a counterphrase. However, if you find the manipulator highlighting a flaw or habit you could easily improve, take constructive steps to address it. This will further help you avoid being vulnerable around them.

These nine psychological techniques are effective in creating a strong foundation for dealing with manipulators and narcissists. It helps you avoid unnecessary arguments, burdensome tasks, and subtly frustrates the manipulator without confrontation. Over time, it makes you seem like an arduous target, causing them to lose interest in manipulating you.

WHEN TO WALK AWAY VS. WHEN TO ENGAGE

Conflict, when handled properly, can yield beneficial outcomes. It can serve a useful purpose and provide opportunities for growth. However, when a conflict arises, our first response is often to get defensive, relying on our basic instincts of fight, flee, or freeze. However, conflicts, when approached mindfully with logic and facts, may reveal that not all of them are motivated by malicious intent.

A conflict arises due to strong emotions that stem from unresolved issues within one or more parties. The best way to decide whether to engage in a conflict or walk away is to focus on your own emotions and regulate them according to the opposing party's demands.

For example, rather than shouting at your slow-witted teammate for ruining the presentation. Stay calm and ask them about their actions, behaviors, or struggles. If you find a specific flaw that the individual could work on, highlight it and ask them to improve on it for future presentations.

Explain the damage it caused to your recent project and how you'd like them to approach similar situations in the future.

Similarly, if you're struggling to manage your anger and frustration over the recent loss. Walk away from the conflict and tell your teammate that you'd like to revisit the issue later. This practice will help you address pressing issues logically, rather than reacting emotionally. The discussions will be more constructive, leading to productive outcomes. You will often notice that the conflict arises simply because of poor communication, misunderstanding, and differences in desired expectations.

Conflicts can arise even when there is no intentional fault on either side. Roles, responsibilities, unclear deadlines, and simply moving from one crisis to another can cause a team or individual to burst out at crucial times. During a crisis, it's important to keep an open mind and agree on a collective solution. Dealing with urgent issues while stressed, frustrated, or burned out often turns trivial matters into heated arguments.

Our bodies respond to conflict by increasing our heart rate, leading to a sudden, illogical, and irrational overreaction to the situation. In hindsight, when the arguments cool off, we often regret our responses. This intense emotional response is known as amygdala hijacking, where the amygdala part of the brain takes over and triggers disproportionate reactions.

When we give ourselves time to process the sudden rise in cortisol, it refines our approach to the situation and helps us formulate logical responses to the argument. There are various ways to manage a conflict, and all of them involve varying degrees of cooperation and assertiveness.

The main five strategies for conflict management are **Avoiding, Accommodating, Competing, Compromising, and Collaborating.**

In the next section, we will further discuss the five conflict strategies and effective tools and techniques, based on an extension from The Pennsylvania State University.

Tools, Techniques & The Five Conflict Management Strategy

There are two kinds of people in a conflict: those who thrive on resolving conflicts with immediate solutions, and those who prefer to step back and revisit issues when the heat has diffused.

The best strategy for approaching a conflict is to understand the seriousness and potential threat of each issue.

For example, when you're experiencing amygdala hijacking, it's advisable to step back and avoid jumping to conclusions until cooler heads prevail. This method is known as the Avoidance Strategy.

The **Accommodating Strategy** is used in situations where the outcome isn't crucial, and a quick decision is important. In this strategy, one party accommodates the other party's needs without asserting their own demands. This strategy is instrumental in building a solid foundation of trust for future collaboration.

The opposite of the Accommodating Strategy is the Competing Strategy. In this method, one should respond assertively and take control of the situation, as the outcome of the conflict plays a crucial role in preventing potential dangers. Being assertive in a heated conflict has a higher chance of cultivating strained relationships, which may be built on negative emotions. However, it helps the team or individual protect their peace of mind and prevent future threats.

The Compromise Strategy differs from the Accommodating Strategy, as both parties need to agree on a neutral solution. Unlike the Accommodating Strategy, both parties must reduce their demands to agree on a prompt decision for the project's fulfillment.

The **Collaboration Strategy** is most effective in situations where both parties have time to resolve personal issues and work together for the project's success, based on trust, effective communication, and complementary skills. The primary focus is to find a solution that benefits both parties.

You can easily switch between strategies as needed, but always make sure to approach the opposing party with respect. Use statements that are humble and polite, rather than condescending. For example, if the conflict arises from your negligence of a trivial matter, there's no harm in apologizing and acknowledging it.

Keeping an open mind, ready to make the other party feel heard, respected, and understood, is key to navigating any conflict toward a mutually fruitful resolution.

Actionable Takeaway

Establish a clear personal space for the manipulator, where they cannot interact or blend with your peers. Enforce firm boundaries and ensure they communicate with you only through their designated channel.

Quick Win

Return all favors promptly and in equal measure to avoid and prevent potential manipulation and larger risks in the future. Keep your focus on the task at hand when a manipulator approaches, so they don't receive your full attention.

CHAPTER 3: HOW TO IDENTIFY A DIFFICULT PERSON

In life, each one of us has occasionally thwarted, annoyed, or confused peers, colleagues, or fellow humans making them put up with our peculiar obsessions and uncompromising attitudes. Although these occasional emotional nuisances make us human, difficult people surpass the boundary by making it their consistent behavior. They don't necessarily set out to pick fights or create chaos now and then, but the way they develop their demeanor, thoughts, words, and actions often leave others around them feeling frustrated, disempowered, or burst into tears of helplessness. In the following subsections, we will learn the common traits of difficult people, categorization as per different personality types, and what steps you must take to cope with the obstinate kind.

Effective coping doesn't necessarily involve acceptance, but rather it aims to balance the power dynamics in your interactions with difficult people. The constructive method to deal with unaccommodating people is not to accept their behavior or engage in futile attempts to change their personality but to neutralize their disruptive tendencies and restore your ability to think critically and act accordingly as per the need of the conflict.

COMMON TRAITS OF DIFFICULT PEOPLE

Every individual on this planet is born with a unique trait, shaped by a combination of experiences, genetics, and upbringing. However, people with difficult personalities often struggle to control their behaviors, actions, and approaches toward threatening circumstances. These patterns of behaviors that disrupt the harmony in workspaces, complicate boundaries, and strain or create friction in personal and professional settings are not necessarily deliberate or malicious, as they often stem from unresolved past issues, trauma, or even innate tendencies of an individual.

Recognizing the root cause is crucial to understanding the twisted pattern in which a difficult individual operates and to equip yourself with effective strategies in dealing with each kind. Here are seven innate qualities or traits that difficult people possess to make workplaces hostile:

CHRONIC NEGATIVITY

Chronic pessimists are quick to point out loopholes in a plan, or hidden problems or seldom acknowledge the solutions or growth of a process. They make it their agenda to highlight every minor mistake and make it an inexorable flaw that hinders the overall progress of the entire team. Having an individual who is blinded by negativity in your team can often lead to unsuccessful projects, stagnation, and a multitude of pending tasks.

To deal with a chronic negative person, you must learn to focus first on the root cause of their negativity that drains energy, dampens morale, and makes collaborative efforts seem futile. Negativity in a person stems from past disappointments or a deep-seated fear of failure due to their unanalyzed actions. This kind of life experience often leads an individual to perceive the world with an over-critical lens.

The best technique to deal with a chronic negative person is by focusing on the underlying issue and acknowledging their viewpoints. Work towards molding their perspective of how the project differs from their failed case and highlight the most beneficial outcomes from it. Emphasize the numbers, facts, figures, and skills that make your project plan failproof from such similar errors that they are highlighting.

Never make the negative person feel that you are dismissing their perspective, rather help them to understand how your strategy could help get rid of their fear of failure.

CONTROL SEEKING BEHAVIORS

Among all the traits of difficult people, this trait is often the most tiresome to tackle as it often arises for two significant reasons: insecurity or lack of trust. Insecurity is a disease that no external act can cure. You could never help a person who doesn't want to help themselves.

Individuals with control-seeking behavior often have an overwhelming need to assert control over situations and others around them. They may go to any extent to align the targeted individual to their agenda. They engage in micromanaging, dominate crucial discussions, dismiss conversations, manipulate through personal threats, and manifest difficult circumstances. These are common acts performed by control-seeking narcissists.

They establish a semblance of order and power in their twisted world, even if it comes at the cost of alienating those around them.

To stand against a manipulative control-seeking individual, you must first understand their motivation for control and redirect their focus toward the tasks that complement their strengths, such as strategic planning.

For example; a control-seeking individual might often suffer from the fear of being inadequate or being strongly judged by others. Praise them for their small wins and try to create an environment of open communication.

Choose your battles wisely, then switch to active listening to dissolve their worries. Once you acknowledge their issues, you will easily be able to diffuse the tension and avoid power struggles. Through assertive communication, a clear boundary, and a task that will channel their behavior into a more positive outlet such as organizing tasks, suggesting or creating the structure of the project will help you manage their negative tendencies effectively. If their behavior becomes repetitive or the addressing of the issues ineffective, limit interactions and seek external support.

Being Defensive or Blame Shifting

The inability to take responsibility for their actions is the hallmark of difficult people. They are skilled at defending themselves and adept at blaming others.

Even though this trait could be quite infuriating, it often arises in individuals due to past experiences of being unfairly judged for their actions. The best way to steer clear of such irresponsible individuals is by keeping and maintaining a detailed track record of your activities, contributions, and involvement in projects. Instead of confronting their false accusations privately or letting them go unchecked, hold them accountable by presenting evidence and addressing the situation with a calm and professional demeanor.

Phrases like: *"I sincerely appreciate your contribution to this project, but I'd like to clarify my role in this situation since I believe there's a misunderstanding between us."* Don't let them dismiss you and stand against them until your point is heard loud and clear by every individual in the room.

UNPREDICTABLE EMOTIONAL OUTBURST

Manipulators are skilled actors of emotional outbursts. When it gets difficult for them to make the targeted individual act in their desired way, they often take refuge in sudden bursts of unresolved emotions. For example, when the targeted individual starts winning the case or debate against the manipulator, the difficult individual may scream, shout, or create a melodramatic scene by crying obnoxiously like a child to divert the victim's mind into handling the tantrum.

They may often link it with some unusual personal issue to make the target feel guilty and get the targeted individual to sympathize and empathize with them. These kinds of manipulative individuals are excellent at crafting believable narratives for their mood swings and unpredictable emotional responses. They may often withdraw without explanation, leaving those around them feeling confused or on edge.

Although there's no strategic method to avoid these emotional manipulators, avoiding excessive contact and reminding them not to mix up personal issues with professional affairs can keep you safe from recurring events.

SARDONIC WIT

Difficult people often resort to sarcasm to mask their intentional procrastination at work. Their tactics may include backhanded compliments, critical remarks, and subtle digs that may leave the targeted individual feeling frustrated and undermined.

The safest strategy to stop letting the manipulator make a mockery of you is by sharpening your replies and being quick at them. If you could anticipate the sarcasm of a manipulator when assigning tasks or requesting updates, arm yourself or stay prepared with sharp thoughtful replies in advance.

For example: A direct yet composed response would be: "I believe you won't

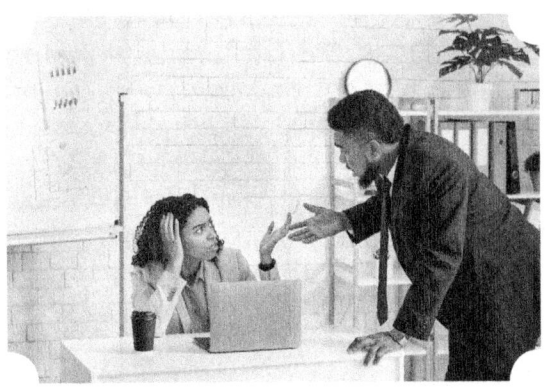

rely on sarcasm to excuse your inefficiency this time."

Sharp witty counterphrases are great for catching the manipulator off guard while maintaining professionalism. If witty responses are not your cup of tea or the manipulator belongs to a higher rank on the corporate scale, stick to assertive communication to calmly redirect the focus to the task at hand.

ENTITLEMENT AND ARROGANCE

Entitled individuals see and believe that all of humanity owes them special treatment. Irrespective of rank or designation, they make sure to project an inflated sense of self-importance over others and force people to treat them like an emperor.

These traits often arise from deep feelings of inadequacy or insecurity. Their inner narcissist thrives by demanding constant attention and belittling others. Their arrogance acts as a shield or an attempt to compensate for their inner struggles, often at the cost of exploiting another person's conscience.

Addressing these traits of a manipulative individual requires a combination of assertiveness, emotional intelligence, and strategic communication.

Foster a team culture that encourages and values equality, collaboration, and accountability. When entitled individuals don't gain traction for their behaviors or words, they often try to adjust, associate, and align with the team norms.

Ask open-ended questions to the entitled individual whenever you are having a one-on-one interaction or team discussion. Questions such as *"How do you think we can balance every individual's contribution in this project to achieve the best results?"* encourage self-introspection in a manipulative individual.

Define boundaries and remind them often not to intrude or prevent them from overstepping. Stay calm and composed when interacting with arrogant individuals, as acting emotionally may transform negotiable issues into threatening arguments.

SINGLE-MINDED PERSPECTIVE

Difficult people lack empathy and the ability to consider other people's perspectives. They often make decisions that solely benefit their agenda or needs and behave unaccommodatingly when asked for reconsideration.

The lack of emotional awareness in difficult people often raises futile conflicts and disagreement within teams, leading to a hostile work environment with decreased morale. Dealing with individuals who lack empathy requires clear communication. Instead of appealing to their emotions or trying to broaden their perspective, use straightforward, logical language and responses.

Explain to them in detail how their self-serving actions impact the entire team's productivity and morale. What consequences do they need to or would be facing if they stay persistent in their self-centered behaviors?

Being selfish at work for staying ahead is a healthy desire, but disregarding other people's crucial needs or turning a blind eye towards the genuine struggles of a team member makes you appear as an uncooperative individual and a person who doesn't value teamwork.

CATEGORIZATION AS PER DIFFERENT PERSONALITIES

Difficult people can often camouflage their behaviors under their dominant personality, making them harder to recognize and address. According to Dr. Robert M. Bramson, the author of *Coping with Difficult People*, workplace archetypes can be differentiated into seven different categories. Learning and understanding how each personality's behavior manifests could offer key insights for recognition and crafting a tailored strategy to deal with each one of them effectively.

Given below is a framework that discusses the dominant behavior of each archetype, their preferred camouflaged personality, key traits to recognize them, and strategy to effectively cope against their tactics, followed by example scenarios.

HOSTILE AGGRESSIVE

These individuals' whole demeanor expresses attack, making you feel inferior by cutting remarks and throwing tantrums. They are arbitrary and often act abusively, abruptly, or intimidatingly to make others see and believe in their perceptions. Their sole motive revolves around making their targeted individual or those around them feel overwhelmed with the power they hold.

Hostile aggressiveness can be spotted attaining positions of authority in the corporate cycle due to their learned ways of attacking people with tantrum-like rage. They hold tremendous power in interpersonal interactions and leave the targeted individual feeling confused with a mental or physical flight.

To avoid being a victim of these manipulative individuals' hostility, you need to first understand the series of emotions the hostile aggressive individuals go through before setting the conflict into flames. For hostile aggressive people, confidence is an ingrained quality in them. They often like to operate independently and straightforwardly and prefer speaking in a clear and concrete manner.

When they perceive or anticipate resistance to their plans, their impatient behaviors quickly turn to irritation, righteous indignation, and rage. They value aggressiveness and confidence, and people who lack these traits are often perceived as weak individuals to be used as props to showcase the power and authority they hold in any situation.

The first effective coping strategy to deal with a hostile aggressive individual is by avoiding confrontation over who is the winner of the argument.

Hostile aggressive people often carry an immense sense of pride. Once they sense an individual is also well capable of fighting back or standing up for themselves, their mind becomes receptive to constructive responses.

Never let yourself be pushed around by aggressive people as doing so will simply make you fade in the scenery. Instead, stand up for yourself with concrete responses to divert the aggressive individual's attention towards you. Oftentimes, when you do stand against their explosive nature or cutting remarks, they may ignore, behave indifferently, or act as if you are nonexistent in the team. But try to indulge them in constructive communication. Constructive communication with polite phrases prevents your acquiescence from being seen as a license for exploitation.

Here are some simple yet effective strategies that you can use to stand up against a hostile aggressive manipulator:

Wait For the Right Moment: Instead of mirroring their demeanor to make your point heard, stay calm and maintain steady eye contact. Keep your stance firm and wait for the yeller to finish. Once they lose momentum in their speech, jump right into the conversations and deliver your solutions.

Break Their Flow of Words: If the manipulator is not calming down with their tantrums for a significant amount of time, cut their conversations with sharp responses that contrast their claims against you.

Refocus Their Attention: When you are standing against a hostile aggressive individual, chances are every move of yours can make them feel threatened and attacked. Keep your demeanor calm and composed. If the person is hostile in their responses, address them with polite assertive phrases like *"I understand your concerns and that is why I decided to discuss this with you first."* This kind of phrase eases their triggered mind and refocuses them to hear you out.

Get Them to Relax: If possible, make the aggressive individual be seated. People are less hostile when they are in a rested position. Use tactful sentences such as *"I believe this discussion will take quite an amount of time, why don't we sit and argue about it comfortably."* Try your best to not let the aggressor be in a standing position for a long time as it will become harder to reach an agreement on a mutual solution.

Highlight Your Point of View: Craft your responses in such a way that does not imply how the opposer should act, behave, think, or talk. Use self-assertive phrases like *"In my opinion, it's a good idea based on the outcome of x"* or *"I understand you don't see that x individual as a good fit for this role, but given the tasks I assigned, he performed exceptionally well."* This response creates an obligation in the manipulator's mind

to consider your point of view rather than concluding solutions based on their sole perspective.

Don't Fight Directly: To keep your budget request fair in the future, don't settle for instant satisfaction. When you stand against an aggressive individual, you practically wage war against them. So, instead of winning the war, win the specific battle to not invite anxiety for future strained relationships.

Hostile aggressive people are often camouflaged as extroverts in your team whose high outgoing energy and confident demeanor might make others hesitant to challenge them on pressing issues. In the case of introverts, they adopt a passive-aggressive tone to undermine their targets subtly.

COMPLAINERS

These individuals are excellent at griping incessantly but never getting any closer to solving a problem. They are loud whiners of workplaces that sing-song about sentences using coordinating conjunctions such as and, also, but, if, etc.

They almost make it impossible for you to overlook them or their perspective as, unlike hostile aggressive individuals, they tend to be cozy and seated in a position because they are aware of the amount of time needed to manipulate you.

These categories of co-workers are non-hostile and could often be spotted as your teammate, group member, or your next desk colleague. They are always unhappy, often about trivial issues, and find fault in every item they encounter. You will often notice the complainers approaching you in a sly, calm demeanor with an unimpressed facial expression and begin their whining while their eyes are continuously wandering around your space to pick up the next nagging item.

For example, let's say you are supposed to review a draft and submit it to the finance department by a given deadline. You've updated the entire team about your previous work priorities and were approved for an extended deadline, but then you catch the complainer of the finance department slowly tracing their steps to your desk.

They would observe you for a complete minute being focused on your task, and then begin their rant while settling beside or in front of you. *"What's the matter? Why do you need an extended deadline? You do understand, right, that even if you were approved for the extended deadline, it does create friction in my team's momentum. And besides, why don't you ever answer my call? I had to provide an important update to you. I know you did reply to my email, but it wouldn't take you long to directly respond to my call. Also, why don't you ever keep your desk arranged? Did you know keeping your workplace tidy boosts your productivity? Speaking of productivity, I hated commuting to work today. I should have taken a leave. The weather calls for a picnic with family. But since you asked for an extended deadline, I couldn't risk taking a leave today."*

Did you see how the complainer skillfully crafted a chain of small talks to make you feel guilty for your pre-approved extended deadline? Complainers should never be confused with a colleague or an individual who has legitimate complaints and wants to bring them to the attention of all the other members.

Unlike complainers, people with genuine problems are focused on finding solutions and receptive to your responses. But a complainer would never be satisfied even if the answer or your solution could resolve the entire issue.

The most perplexing nature of a skilled complainer is how they use subtle truths to ramble their accusations; they do so to make you feel helpless to shut them up. They stay updated and keep track of your and your team members' weaknesses and charge you against them. As a result, you feel uncertain about your decisions, drained and exhausted after every interaction.

To effectively cope with a complainer, you must first learn to identify the real underlying issue. In each conflict, every complainer visualizes themselves as powerless, prescriptive, and perfect. Their real agenda is to get you to comply and fix a mistake for them that might or might not be yours.

Here's how you should approach a complainer to reshape their three perspectives about themselves:

Powerless: Every human develops a unique perspective about things they believe they can control in their life and things they consider out of their control. Complainers fall into the category of individuals who believe every mishap, unfairness, or problem that arises in their life is caused by an external force. They are victims of outer circumstances, and there's nothing they could do or no one to hear their cries. They are often poor at managing crucial issues and gripe about every trivial complication.

For example, a complainer might shirk their required work hours needed for maintaining a higher rank in key performance indicators, yet blame the supervisor or boss for a lack of acknowledgment due to an insignificant disagreement that happened last winter.

Prescriptive: "Prescriptive" means having strong opinions about how things should be. Complainers hold a strong sense of opinion about every aspect of life and behave inflexibly when things don't go as they want them to. You might often find a complainer grumbling against the messy habits of one of your team members, and yet instead of holding them accountable or asking them directly to mend their ways, they will cry and whine to you, making your working hours equally unproductive. Unlike individuals who genuinely believe or perceive things as out of their control, complainers trap themselves in the loop of constant unfairness by focusing on how they desire things to be and how they turn out in reality.

Perfect: Since complainers often point out real problems, they often shirk responsibility in two specific steps. First, by observing the flaws and how they impact the entire team. Second, by highlighting how they brought the matter to your attention. It's their favorite and most preferred way of self-validating their righteous behavior.

Once the complainer completes highlighting their issue to you, it's never an issue for them to resolve. You are the one accountable for finding a solution and dealing with the uncalled problem. They make you appear as sinners if you ignore their words and construct a vacuum of crafted complaints that slowly but steadily eat up your conscience.

The key to successfully breaking a complainer's self-confirming righteous cycle is by eradicating them of these three factors: Power, Prescriptive, and Perfect.

Here's a step-by-step process of how to reshape a complainer's perspective.

Become an Attentive Listener: Being attentive to a complainer is an arduous task, especially if the entire discussion is about a third person. Complainers often have a favorite target to exploit or whine about. They are obsessed with them and take years to move on to another individual unless compelled by an external factor such as a job shift.

Attentive listening is a powerful interpersonal tool that, when used strategically, can make you skilled at handling difficult people. There are four primary reasons why you should listen to a complainer.

a. Helps the complainer calm down, making them receptive to your responses.

b. Not being dismissed for their responses prevents triggering a greater outpouring of complaints.

c. Attentive listening will provide you with key information to resolve the conflict immediately.

d. Surprisingly, sometimes you may notice that the complainer is either finding a solution by themselves or just needs a sympathetic ear to share their overwhelming emotions.

Paraphrase Their Whining: Instead of dismissing their complaints, identify the core issue or information that triggered an hour of griping and form your response around addressing it. For example, if a colleague from the finance department complains about the delayed draft, you could paraphrase their concerns by saying:

"It seems like you're frustrated because you weren't able to update me personally over the phone. How about this: Moving forward, let's prioritize email for work-related updates. I check my email more regularly during work hours, which will allow for quicker responses without relying on phone distractions."

Personalize your responses by using their preferred name and deliver them thoughtfully. This subtly reinforces your boundaries while acknowledging their input.

Interrupt the Complainer: Complainers love to talk, and their statements can go on endlessly with a series of conjunctions. The best way to stop them is to understand the core issue and limit your responses by focusing only on the solution to the main problem. Avoid acknowledging any irrelevant details that don't help resolve the issue.

Avoid Agreeing: Unlike acknowledgment, agreeing with a complainer can lead to an endless loop of verbal back-and-forth. While it's true that your delayed review of the draft might slow down the momentum of the finance department, agreeing with such a broad accusation can lead to future re-accusations. Validation can only make them feel blameless and powerless in the situation.

Don't Ask Why: When switching to problem-solving mode with complainers, avoid asking why the problem exists. Instead, ask what they could have done differently or how they would like to address the issue. This shifts their mindset from complaints to constructive responses. Once you know the involved parties, the date, time, and details, encourage the complainer to suggest solutions. This often helps them find the answer themselves without needing your direct intervention.

Make Them Outline Their Issues: When you ask a complainer to write down their problem, you resolve half of the issue. Why? Because no complainer focuses on just one issue. They are constantly on the lookout for things to bicker about. By requesting that a complainer put their concerns in writing or by saying something like, *"Sylvia, I have an important meeting at 10:30 am, and it's currently 10:20 am. What conclusion would you prefer us to reach in the next 10 minutes?"* you create a sense of urgency that encourages them to focus on the key issues.

If they complain about you being unavailable or busy, politely ask them to send you an email or message with all their viewpoints. It's highly unlikely that a complainer will take the time to detail every trivial issue in writing.

Complainers often camouflage themselves as ambiverts, adjusting their personalities based on the energy of the person they're targeting. They blend into the individual's preferred productive hours and make their squabbling seem justified.

SILENT UNRESPONSIVE

These individuals put you in a limbo of short, unproductive responses. Even if you propose a plan that could save your company a significant amount of money in production, their responses are always limited to yes, no, or a grunt. They make you feel guilty for expecting a reasonable response, acting as though offering you even a sentence of words is a burden, as if they'd have to pay double tax for doing so.

People who are generally quiet differ from silent unresponsive individuals because they don't avoid acknowledging or replying when asked directly. Sometimes, an individual may not contribute to an issue because they have nothing productive to add. To differentiate between someone with fewer words and a non-verbal manipulator, pay attention to the nonverbal cues that the manipulator often displays.

There are three types of unresponsive manipulators who are the most infuriating in a workplace:

The Noncommittal Ones: These individuals avoid committing to anything because they fear the consequences of being held accountable. They might think, *"If I agree and the conflict arises, you'll consider me irresponsible and perhaps reprimand me or not assign me any other tasks. It's better to stay quiet and let you figure out the solution."* These types of unresponsive individuals always avoid handling potentially painful interpersonal interactions.

The Calculated Aggressor: These manipulative individuals take pleasure in seeing the frustration of others. They withhold key information just to make a mockery of the situation and assert their dominance over others. One of their favorite tactics is to intentionally put up a stone face in the face of adversity, relishing the torment they cause their targets.

The Intentional Clueless: These individuals use silence as a defense mechanism. They think, *what good would come from sharing this key piece of information? It's better to act oblivious and* *let others fill in the gaps to avoid addressing the issue.* These types of unresponsive individuals have a deep-seated fear that sharing their genuine problems would make them vulnerable to exploitation. Rather than tackling issues constructively and collaboratively, they sweep everything under the "silent rug," leaving others to deal with it.

According to Dr. Robert M. Bramson, there are two basic types of non-verbal cues that these unresponsive individuals use against their targets:

The Frowning: When a silent unresponsive manipulator disagrees with you, you may notice their forehead covered with frown lines, their eyes squinting, their nose scrunching, and their entire face masked by a scowl.

Of course, it might not always be as vivid, since silent unresponsive individuals tend to avoid overly animated expressions. However, if you pay close attention, you may pick up on subtle cues, such as a furrowed brow or a blank stare devoid of emotion.

The Subtle Gestures: These individuals use body language to communicate the meanings behind their withdrawn behaviors. Gestures like shaking a fist to express anger, crossing their arms to signal defensiveness, or giving a thumbs-up to prompt you to repeat your entire plan over and over again are common actions.

Although gestures are generally considered a form of acknowledgment with standardized meanings, they can

leave you confused and frustrated due to cultural differences and the context of the situation.

The most effective way to cope with a silent unresponsive manipulator is by compelling them to speak. Here are some strategies to get these individuals talking:

Always Ask Open-Ended Questions: When engaging with a silent unresponsive individual, avoid general questions like, *"Do you agree?"* or *"Would you like to add anything?"* These types of questions allow them to dismiss the issue with a simple yes or no. Instead, craft questions that invite them to share their viewpoints, such as *"What's your method of resolving the issue?"* or *"What difficulties are you facing due to the ongoing conflict?"*

Let the Silence Amplify: If you're dealing with a skilled non-responder, even after asking a reflective or open-ended question, you may receive a grunt or "nothing" in response, followed by a long, painful pause. Don't fill the silence with your own response just because their demeanor makes you feel awkward. Instead, maintain your friendly, open-to-constructive-criticism demeanor and wait for them to reply.

Make Them Focus on the Present Moment: If you don't receive a response for a significant amount of time, redirect their focus to the surrounding silence. Keep your tone as polite as possible and use open-ended questions, such as, *"I expected a reasonable response from you, yet you're choosing to stay quiet. May I please* know what's troubling you about sharing your thoughts?" Give them enough time to respond. If they don't, ask another open-ended question.

Break the Tension: Instead of being intimidated by their icy stare and cold demeanor, break the tension by asking genuine questions, such as, *"Could you please help me understand why you're choosing to remain quiet and not share your views?"* Be prepared to receive a yes or no in response, which may further frustrate you.

However, do not let your dissatisfaction show on your face. The person is well aware of the emotions they are feeling and may later realize your viewpoints once they've calmed down.

Take the Solid Satisfying Step: If none of your efforts bear fruit and the individual continues to stay silent, use assertive responses to conclude the meeting by highlighting the inefficiency of the time spent. You could say something like, *"Well, we all invested an hour discussing this potential issue, and since we didn't find any answers today, I will be rescheduling the meeting for tomorrow as this is an important project for my team."* If the follow-up meeting still doesn't yield productive outcomes, inform the individual of the steps you'll need to take to complete the project and the decisions you'll have to make independently. Keep a record of all discussions to avoid unnecessary blame.

Silent unresponsive individuals often camouflage themselves as introverts, using their deliberate silence as a trait of thoughtfulness or being reserved.

SUPER AGREEABLE

The super agreeable category of people is always reasonable, sincere, and supportive to your face but will never deliver on a promise. They always wear a smile, appear friendly, make you laugh, and agree with every reasonable request or plan you propose.

You can never spot a concrete hurdle when dealing with them, as they will always give you a satisfying reply and suggest better solutions to your problems. But when it comes time to put the discussed plans into action, they will ghost you and leave you on their waiting list.

There's just one reason why these pseudo-yes-yellers behave this way: **Instant Affection**. From an early age, they learn that people are drawn to someone with a good sense of humor, someone who makes them feel okay, heard, and understood. Super agreeable people are skilled at making others believe that their very presence brightens up their otherwise mundane work lives.

Their innate nature of avoiding conflict has short-term benefits, but these are often gained at a long-term high cost. To cope with a super agreeable person, you first need to make them believe that honesty is non-threatening.

Super agreeable individuals manipulate the presentation of reality to gain your approval. So, if you want a super agreeable person to tell you the truth, you must make their criticism feel accepted and valued. Just like a parent might use soft parenting to avoid threatening their child, you need to request a straightforward response from a super agreeable person for their honest opinion.

Here are some phrases that can help you convince a super agreeable person to speak their mind:

Instead of asking, *"What didn't you like about my presentation?"* say, *"I'm really glad you liked my presentation, but every presentation has parts that are better than others. Which part do you think stands out the most in my presentation?"*

If the person still feels threatened to share their honest opinions, or fears that you might start disliking them, they will likely respond with something like, *"I believe every part of your presentation is great. You discussed and highlighted all the crucial points that needed to be known."* Never let them finish the discussion without adding your words. Repeat, *"Thank you so much; I value our friendship, which is why I wanted to know your honest opinions. I'm glad you're not holding back any key information. I have the time to go over the parts that aren't up to par. What do you suggest?"*

Adding these specific words creates subtle pressure on the super agreeable person while reassuring them at the same time. They will point out what's outstanding in your report, if not the parts that could use improvement. This way, you'll have something to work with instead of facing a complete rejection in the future.

The super agreeable person tends to camouflage themselves as both extroverts and introverts. They use their extroverted qualities to charm their way out of accountability, relying on likability and avoiding follow-through or confrontation by using their introverted traits of agreeableness.

NEGATIVIST

The negativist at work comes with a set of responses designed to drain your morale and make you believe that none of your productive suggestions will work. Their responses to any proposed plan often include:

- "No, it won't work."

- "We've tried that idea before."

- "There's nothing productive you can reap from this situation."

- "This is a lost cause."

- "The higher-ups will never agree."

Even responses like, *"Yes, we could think it over later sometime,"* or *"Let's consider your idea for the next project,"* are met with skepticism. The negativist harbors an innate belief that no solution, absolutely nothing, can resolve their misery, and every team member must simply accept the status quo. If you ask, *"What do you suggest then?"* be prepared to be met with an almost inaudible, *"Nothing,"* effectively ending the conversation.

Negativists are skilled at using conversation stoppers, deploying them with such conviction that you may start to believe that you were simply over-optimistic about your ideas, and none of them are fruitful. To cope effectively with a negativist at work, you must first recognize your vulnerability and be aware of how easily they can tap into your disappointment.

Your next step is to counter their negativity with concrete past examples, situations, or wins that contradict their pessimistic viewpoint. If you can't recall any immediately, buy yourself time by saying, *"Well, if you think that higher-ups' approval could be a problem, I'll try re-proposing the plan to them once again. There's no harm in a second attempt."* The negativist might try to convince you that your effort will be unproductive, but take control of the conversation by replying, *"Well, it's better than doing absolutely nothing."*

Another effective technique is to avoid presenting the entire plan to them upfront. Knowing that their negative outlook will drain your morale, don't rush to propose solutions right away. Instead, save the presentation of solutions until the problem has been thoroughly discussed.

Negativists resist change and dismiss ideas. In a workplace, they may camouflage themselves as ambiverts, balancing their negativity with critique, which helps mask their resistance to change.

KNOW-IT EXPERTS

In the professional world, there are two kinds of know-it-all experts: the one who has concrete ideas and is exceptional at their work, and the other who doesn't. Regardless of the depth of knowledge they possess, both types want you to believe they know everything there is to know about the subject and how the world works.

The first type of know-it-all expert, those who have concrete ideas, are highly productive individuals. They exude power and dominance, operating on competent, carefully crafted plans. They are often independent workers to such an extent that they make those around them almost invisible.

This one flaw — not being able to adjust to other people's ideas or solutions — is what earns them a place in the book of difficult people. You may often feel condescended to, belittled, inept, confused, and stupid, fostering deep resentment toward a know-it-all expert. Indeed, they are factually correct 80% of the time, but the remaining 20% is a disaster when highlighted by another party or if their plan fails.

Know-it-all experts should never be confused with genuine subject matter experts, as the main difference lies in their method of communication. A subject matter expert is always open to new ideas and remains humble about their knowledge, whereas know-it-all experts see little need to listen to others and respond with irritation, outright anger, or withdrawal when confronted with differing opinions, viewing them as personal contradictions rather than other people's interpretations of facts.

The first strategy to get a know-it-all expert to agree with your viewpoints is by doing your homework.

If you want them to consider alternative solutions, you must communicate articulately, emphasizing the facts, figures, and benefits that could be gained from your proposed plan. Be very attentive when interacting with a know-it-all expert, as there are high chances you will learn more than you expect after convincing them to discuss your ideas and presenting yourself as someone who values knowledge. Know-it-all experts respect people who have a hunger for learning.

Use a polite questioning tone rather than an authoritative tone to seek answers to your doubts or highlight issues, such as: *"I'm having a little difficulty understanding how your proposed plan would help us resolve this issue in particular,"* or *"How do you envision the progress of the project and the growth of the company by applying that particular method?"* or *"Are there any other alternatives that you believe could have worked for this crisis?"* Know-it-all experts love playing the role of work dictionaries. The better you are at articulating your

thoughts and demonstrating your knowledge, the more welcomed you will be in their circle.

Now, let's talk about how to effectively cope with the other kind of expert, the one who presents themselves as knowledgeable but, in reality, isn't.

These are the people who suddenly gain a great amount of power or wealth without any previous hardships or accurate knowledge. They are always dismissive of your remarks and believe they are factually correct almost all of the time. There is no 80/20 ratio with these people; they always have little to no knowledge about the subject but behave as though they are the sole bearers of knowledge. Working with this type is risky, as it often results in and risks causing significant damage.

To effectively cope with such phony individuals, simply state facts and truths as your own perceptions. Phony know-it-all experts often feel immobilized when confronted with real knowledge. Help them save face by steering the conversation using phrases like, *"Well, I think you meant that solving the conflict by [input your specified idea] would be worth a try."*

Know-it-all experts dominate discussions, dismissing others' input to showcase superiority. Camouflaging as an extrovert helps them use their charisma to monopolize the conversation. In the case of an introverted know-it-all, they often rely on technical expertise and speak only to correct others or assert dominance.

INDECISIVENESS

The truth about indecisive people is that they will never let you take control of a situation, nor will they make any positive or negative remarks until it solely benefits them. They have a peculiar eye for perfection that can never be achieved, which leads to pending projects and unexecuted plans.

Ironically, indecisive people—those who constantly swing back and forth between two alternative decisions—have a strong desire to be helpful toward others. However, this desire often makes them frustrating.

"However I decide, someone will not like it. I don't want to deliberately hurt anybody. I cannot knowingly make a decision or be a part of something that might cause a rift between teams." These individuals prefer sitting still with the problem rather than making a decision that may or may not raise initial tension.

What makes them even more frustrating is that their approval often plays a crucial part in executing your proposed plan. So how do they avoid hurting the person who proposed the plan? They simply delay their decision until the very last minute. The longer they wait, the fewer people will approach them, or others will forget about it altogether.

There is only one effective way to cope with an indecisive person and get them to make a decision: set a deadline and give them two concrete options. For example,

if you have already proposed the details of a plan and the indecisive individual has yet to provide their feedback, schedule another meeting, highlighting the urgency of the matter. You can say, *"We have to decide before next Thursday. Let me know which solution you prefer between option A and option B."*

Keep your tone friendly but firm so that the indecisive person does not feel attacked. In the workplace, they often camouflage themselves as ambiverts, masking their indecisive nature with consideration for others and switching accordingly to keep creating bottlenecks and delaying progress.

HOW TO RECOGNIZE TOXIC BEHAVIOR PATTERNS AND WARNING SIGNS

Now that we have learned and understood the seven types of workplace archetypes, let's decode the key traits that serve as warning signs for each type.

Hostile-Aggressive: Hostile, aggressive people often display behaviors such as loud interruptions, dismissive remarks, and critical, condescending behavior, both in private and in public.

Complainers: Complainers tend to focus persistently on obstacles rather than solutions, masking their negativity with pseudo-criticism using phrases like, "I'm

just being truthful and realistic."

Super Agreeables: Super agreeable individuals eagerly agree to every task or request, but consistently make excuses when they fail to deliver.

Silent-Unresponsive: These individuals avoid eye contact or verbal responses, frequently using silence as a defense mechanism.

Negativists: People who fall under the negativist category often have a pessimistic outlook and frequently point out flaws without suggesting improvements. They tend to frame their resistance as concern or pragmatism.

Know-It-All Experts: Know-it-all experts often interrupt conversations to assert their knowledge and react defensively when challenged.

Indecisive: Indecisive individuals frequently seek reassurance before agreeing to a choice and tend to revisit finalized decisions.

Actionable Takeaway

Identify and recognize the subtle cues of each type of manipulator to establish specific boundaries that discourage them from pursuing you.

Quick Win

Always speak assertively when dealing with a manipulator.

CHAPTER 4: HOW TO ESTABLISH CREDIBILITY WITHOUT RESORTING TO FLATTERY

In life, we often encounter people who praise us for every decision we make, telling us how smart, wise, and brave we are. *"That's a great decision! What a nice suit! What an expensive car!"*—and the list never ends. But among these genuine well-wishers, there are some individuals who blur the line between compliments and over-praising.

They make you feel pleased, important, and attractive by any means necessary, all to get you to agree with their agenda.

The most common flattery we encounter in everyday life tends to happen in our workplaces, and the prime targets of these pseudo-compliments are our bosses or those in positions of authority.

It's raise season, but I'm still falling short of meeting my KPIs. Enter flattery. The boss has second thoughts—let's boost his ego with compliments. The new manager is in charge of promotions; cue the flattery. An attractive colleague walks in—don't stop showering her with praise.

Every human enjoys basking in the adoration of others, but when you encourage people to speak freely, you limit the opportunities for them to conspire against you over issues they want to pursue. ~ Han Fei Tzu, as mentioned in The Municipal Machiavelli.

It's hard to recognize genuine admiration in a world where a compliment here and a glowing remark there often feel like a calculated move accompanied by a rehearsed smile. Beneath every praise lingers a whisper of doubt, prompting us to question the real motive of the person. Establishing credibility without resorting to flattery requires sincerity, courage, authenticity, and, most importantly, emotional intelligence.

Every business has witnessed stories where a highly intelligent and highly skilled executive is removed from a leadership position, only to fail miserably. On the other hand, someone with no extraordinary knowledge and basic technical abilities may be elevated to a similar position and soar.

This is not a case of overnight growth, nor is there any enchanted element involved in gaining what you deserve. Rather, it's a series of steps you must consider to avoid violating boundaries when dealing with a difficult boss.

HOW TO DEAL WITH A DIFFICULT BOSS WITHOUT VIOLATING BOUNDARIES

Throughout our careers, we work with many bosses. Some treat you and assign tasks based on your potential, while others forget that they lead a team of humans, not machines. Both good and bad bosses have personality traits, quirks, and habits that can either be redeeming or frustrating. For each type, tactfully addressing your issues is key to keeping your bills paid for a longer period.

Before learning how to deal with various types of difficult bosses, you must first master how to communicate in a constructive and non-threatening manner. Here are some basic rules to remember when attempting to resolve a conflict between you and your boss:

- Don't react—act. Approach your boss with assertiveness.

- Use constructive criticism as a tool for communication, not a weapon to challenge your boss.

- Keep your tone polite and respectful.

- State facts, not assumptions or feelings.

- Use examples and previous cases to support your points.

- Focus on solving the problem, not proving who's right.

- If your boss's personality is too intimidating to handle, seek help from a neutral party to ease the tension.

- Avoid burning bridges; find a way to cross them.

Every boss has idiosyncratic behaviors and unique communication quirks. The best way to err on the side of caution is to learn how to navigate each of them. If you can easily ignore or work around negative remarks without affecting the quality of your productivity, stay focused on your work and do a good job. However, if certain habits or behaviors impact your work or attitude to the point where you become unproductive or stagnant, speak up and confront your boss.

Confronting your boss is quite different from dealing with a coworker or colleague. While you can apply the techniques and methods you learned in the previous chapters to resolve a conflict with your boss, don't forget the supreme power they hold over you. They may have the authority or control over the resources that fund your wages and keep you employed.

Approaching your boss in a conflict requires greater sensitivity and tact. The first step in resolving a conflict is always to view the situation from your boss's perspective. The quicker you adopt their point of view, the easier it will be to find a resolution.

The Six Archetypes of Bosses and How to Deal with Each One

Abusive Boss

Abusive bosses are bullies; they are often similar to hostile, aggressive individuals. They have the potential to berate you for even the smallest reasons. To deal with an abusive boss, you first need to build your confidence to confront them and stop the abuse in its tracks. Don't let your boss shout at you, only to retreat and sulk in private. Instead, call them out on their explosive behavior.

For Example: Imagine you're an employee working at a supermarket. Your boss assigns you the task of rearranging the shelves in the 5th aisle after some customers' children left it in disarray. As you begin arranging the items, a customer approaches you for help. You assist them with directions, but before you can return to your task, another customer approaches with a different query. Since you can't find any teammates to redirect them to, you spend a significant amount of time helping the customer.

When you finally return to your assigned task, your boss arrives, notices the unfinished shelves, and starts shouting at you in front of customers. The situation makes everyone uncomfortable, as your boss lacks discretion and tact. Instead of standing idly by and letting your boss's sharp remarks affect you, redirect their focus to the customers.

Be loud and clear in voicing your viewpoints, and make them aware of how their behavior is creating a hostile environment for customers within earshot. Politely ask them to address work-related matters in the office, rather than in front of the entire store, as it damages the store's reputation. Maintain a calm and confident demeanor. If your boss is generally reasonable but suffers from occasional outbursts, offer a listening ear and try to understand if there is another pressing issue causing their anxiety. You might be surprised to find that, most of the time, their anger is directed at an entirely different matter.

Abusive bullies cannot be transformed into tactful, courteous bosses overnight, but they can be more easily handled when you respond to them with a contrasting demeanor.

Controlling Boss

Controlling bosses are close relatives of know-it-all experts, but they take it a step further by assigning unreasonable amounts of work without considering your existing schedule. However, there's another side to this behavior. Your boss might genuinely have unavoidable responsibilities to handle. They may be burdened with excessive work or simply don't have the time to hold meetings or discuss suggestions. It's often easier to tell others what to do than to ask for opinions, wait for responses, and adjust accordingly.

The controlling nature of a boss usually arises for two key reasons:

a. They are new to the role and need time to learn how to manage and trust employees with the tasks assigned.

b. They feel validated by the power they have while being in control of others.

Being in control is part of every boss's personality, and attempting to change this behavior is futile. It will only add to your stress and invite unnecessary trouble. The best way to deal with a controlling boss is by approaching them with a friendly, polite demeanor.

For Example: Imagine your boss walking up to your desk and leaving a pile of work for you to complete within a short time frame. Instead of complaining about how many other responsibilities you need to prioritize, show them all the projects you're currently handling and ask for a solution. Question them about how they would like you to approach and prioritize each task to meet their deadline. You may be surprised to find that, most of the time, your controlling boss doesn't realize the

full scope of your workload and may even help you reassign some of those tasks.

Egotistical Boss

Egotistical bosses exhibit two distinct characteristics: they love basking in the glory of others' achievements while always blaming others for failures. You can never expect a constructive conversation with them, as any matter becomes a threat to their fragile, glorified sense of self.

When you voice your concerns to an egotistical boss, they often perceive it as the entire team scheming against them, which only worsens the situation. The best way to deal with an egotistical boss is to first stroke their ego and then address the main issue.

For Example: Imagine your egotistical boss asks you to complete a presentation because your skills have always impressed higher-ups. At first, you don't mind them taking credit, as you are still learning and growing within the company. However, when you make a mistake on a project, they shift the entire blame onto you in front of your coworkers. Instead of tolerating this unfair treatment, confront your egotistical boss by first acknowledging their contributions, then highlighting the issue.

Here's an example of what you might say:

"I'm grateful to you for aligning me with such great opportunities. However, as my leader, you've never guided me or offered praise when a project was successful, nor suggested

improvements for tasks I've submitted. I've always had to guess whether I did a good job by seeing you take the credit. We're a team. If you continue blaming me for mistakes in front of my superiors, please let me know when I do a good job as well. It would help me understand how to work with you more effectively, so you never have to experience this frustration again. I would never want to present a half-done report, but if you don't voice your compliments the way you voice blame, it's demotivating and leaves me confused for future projects."

This approach works because it consistently shifts the attention to benefit the egotistical boss. They don't like taking responsibility for failures, and this dialogue plants the seed that they need to acknowledge your successes for their benefit. Some egotistical bosses feel threatened by your efficiency and become excessively competitive. The most effective way to deal with an insecure boss is to praise their work and small victories, helping them see you as an ally rather than a threat.

Incompetent Boss

Working under an incompetent boss who lacks leadership or managerial skills can actually be an opportunity if you learn how to fill in the gaps between their abilities and the demands of the project. Rather than complaining about your boss's lack of qualifications for the role, help them complete tasks and secure the

necessary outcomes. This not only helps you manage your negative emotions towards the situation but also earns your boss's unwavering trust. An employee who makes things easier for a boss who is new and lacks experience will be valued more than someone who works against the new boss or tries to prove they're better.

We all start as trainees, and we all lack skills in some areas of our lives. When you choose to be a supportive friend to your incompetent boss, helping them learn new skills and manage their work, you open up opportunities for your own growth. Your boss will likely come to rely on you, mention your name in important board meetings, or suggest you make key decisions that contribute to the company's success.

Inconsistent Boss

This type of boss behaves like they're on a pendulum. One minute they shower you with praise, and the next, they make you question your worth. Working with an inconsistent boss can be exhausting if you don't develop a thick skin towards their fluctuating mood. This kind of boss treats everyone the same way, so it's often not about you or your work, but rather their mood that dictates how they acknowledge your productivity. On days when your boss is grumpy or annoyed, limit your interaction and focus on highlighting your progress rather than raising problems. However, if a critical decision must be made despite their mood, confront them politely and ask genuine questions.

For Example: If your boss complains about the same project they praised just the day before, without any changes, ask them what caused their shift in opinion overnight. Be transparent about your feelings and seek guidance, emphasizing how understanding their emotions better will be beneficial for both of you. You may be surprised to learn that the issue is often unrelated to work or stems from an external influence.

This approach will help you better manage your boss's unpredictable nature in future projects and preserve your sanity from unnecessary stress.

Unethical Boss

Unethical bosses disregard company policies and bend the rules to suit their needs. They often lie, cheat, and are skilled at distorting the truth. Their behavior can extend to unlawful activities like padding expenses, taking office supplies, stealing money, or shifting the blame to employees.

Working for an unethical boss is difficult because you are forced to sit idly while they engage in actions that contradict your morals, ethics, and the company's policies. You may love your job, but the burden of being an unwitting accomplice can weigh heavily on you.

Confronting an unethical boss requires careful judgment. You need to evaluate whether addressing their questionable behavior is worth your time and energy, or if it's better to let it go and focus on your own priorities.

However, if your unethical boss forces you to become complicit, highlight the consequences of their actions. Help them understand how it will negatively impact your work, career trajectory, and well-being. If you are able and willing, offer a solution that genuinely addresses the problem rather than covering it up with more lies.

For Example: Imagine your manager asks you to manipulate audit numbers to protect the store's reputation with higher-ups. Instead of agreeing out of fear of losing your job, approach them with a solution-oriented mindset. Point out the long-term consequences they may face if you comply, and explain how it could damage the store's credibility and erode trust among employees. Suggest an alternative approach, such as how you and your team could communicate the challenges you've faced and collaborate with higher-ups to improve the numbers in the next sales cycle.

HOW TO MAKE A TEAM THRIVE WITH CHALLENGING COLLEAGUES

Keeping one difficult colleague in a team of skilled individuals is like placing a rotten apple in a basket of fresh fruits. You can never expect the other fruits to stay fresh for long, as the flies will eat up the fresher ones before they finish the rot. In the case of humans, one or more difficult co-workers in a team can derail the entire project. You can never expect any productivity from them and will be the sole bearer of every responsibility just so they can later take advantage of your hard work.

To effectively deal with challenging colleagues and make your team thrive in every project, you need to focus on defining responsibilities for each individual. Learn about the key traits of each worker and assign them tasks that they won't whine about. For example, people who don't like to be involved in discussions or use silence as their guard could be good at technical expertise. In that case, assign them non-verbal tasks that will keep them engaged in producing results.

Provide clear, definite instructions and outline the expectations of the outcomes along with the consequences if they fail to comply. When you set predefined rules and regulations, you create boundaries for those who unnecessarily whine about work and also force individuals to speak up about genuine roadblocks.

Stay prepared for uncalled setbacks or rough weather, as most difficult people are likely to spend time plotting against the project's failure rather than working productively toward it. One effective solution to deal with such a nuisance is by highlighting the benefit each individual could reap from the success of the project, keeping all team members and coworkers focused on the end goal.

Thriving in a team consisting of difficult colleagues is much harder than it seems. It's better to address the issue at the management level by establishing non-negotiable guidelines during the hiring process. A behavioral interview could help uncover the red flags of a candidate, such as why they were dismissed from their previous job, along with a thorough background check. Assumptions made solely based on personality and past mistakes should be avoided, and reflective questions should be asked to decode the true talent of the soon-to-be-recruited person.

Building a team that consists of members who complement each other's strengths and weaknesses is far better and more functional than creating a team that solely focuses on elevating strong individuals.

STRATEGIES AND TECHNIQUES TO PROSPER WITHOUT SUPPORT

The first step to prospering without support in your job or continuing a familial role in your work life is building resilience.

Whether you are trying to navigate your way through office politics, catch up on your pending tasks, or simply work without inviting unnecessary attention, resilience toward any uncalled situation, combined with your ability to adapt to new challenges, determines your success for the future.

It's difficult to thrive in a work environment where everyone is either unresponsive or pays a deaf ear to your genuine issues, but choosing to thrive in an unsupportive environment can easily transform it into a platform for your growth and success. You just need to develop a learning attitude.

The most rewarding result of thriving without support is learning and recognizing your unique leadership style and expanding its approach. As mentioned in the book *The Power of Emotional Intelligence*, written by Daniel Goleman, leaders who master at least four styles of leadership create the best work climate and business performance.

They make leadership fluid by pre-determining the success and cohesion of a team, emphasizing the unique impact and relevance toward the goals of the project and company. Here is a descriptive outline of the five distinct leadership styles, their impact on the work environment, how they help build resonance, and in what scenarios you should consider applying them.

Visionary Leadership: Visionary leadership provides direction and clarity when a team struggles with unanticipated changes or uncertainty. These leaders inspire others by focusing on shared dreams and mutual goals, guiding them toward a secure future. It builds trust and cultivates innovation by aligning each individual's contributions with the larger organizational goals. Since visionary leaders encourage collaboration and creativity, this style is best exercised during transitions to help employees embrace change with a sense of redefined purpose.

Coaching Leadership: Coaching leadership prioritizes individual growth through frequent sessions that help team members connect and collaborate effectively. It focuses on aligning personal aspirations with project goals and how individuals can grow from completing them. This approach cultivates a sense of belonging, which nurtures talent, boosts morale, and fosters a culture of continuous learning. It also plays a significant role in attracting and retaining top talent within teams.

Affiliative Leadership: Affiliative leadership operates by strengthening interpersonal connections and cultivating trust and camaraderie among team members. This style is instrumental in resolving conflicts, healing rifts, and creating a supportive environment where each team member feels valued and heard. Affiliative leaders often step in during critical times to motivate and remind members of previous successes to boost team morale.

Democratic Leadership: Democratic leadership promotes accountability and fosters an inclusive, empowered work culture. It is particularly useful when creativity and diverse perspectives are essential to the success of a project. These leaders encourage commitment and ensure that every team member's voice is heard to make well-informed decisions.

Pacesetting Leadership: Pacesetting leadership sets ambitious goals and expects high-quality results from top teams or competent individuals. These leaders lead by example, with a strong work ethic and a drive for extraordinary success in projects. However, despite their excellence, this leadership style can often be perceived negatively, as employees may feel pressured and overwhelmed, leading to burnout and suppressed resentment. To avoid creating a negative atmosphere, pacesetting leaders must balance their high expectations with clear guidelines that enable the team to operate efficiently.

Commanding or Coercive Leadership: This style provides clear direction during emergencies and crises, helping individuals navigate potential pitfalls by commanding the exact steps needed to achieve a goal. However, it is often associated with a negative approach due to its potential for misuse by manipulators. Commanding or coercive leadership is best applied during decision fatigue or high-stress situations to kickstart growth or stabilize a chaotic, nonfunctional environment.

Whenever you find yourself struggling to find support in a work environment, approach your work with any of the six leadership mindsets mentioned to turn a crisis into an opportunity. However, always keep in mind not to overuse the negatively perceived leadership styles, as they may backfire and establish you as a threat to other team members.

CHAPTER 5: THE ART OF NON-VERBAL ASSERTIVENESS

Non-verbal communication is the unspoken language your body uses to convey the intentions and emotions behind the words you choose to speak. It includes gestures, postures, facial expressions, eye movements, and brow movements. When used effectively, these non-verbal cues can enhance your communication. The way you use non-verbal communication on a daily basis has a direct impact on how others perceive you, and if your non-verbal cues don't align with your verbal messages, they can cause confusion.

To become a better communicator, it's crucial to pay attention to matching your actions with your words. This increases trust, clarity, and rapport, amplifying the five roles of body language to build strong, rewarding relationships.

Here are the five roles of body language, along with examples, to help you understand their importance in the workplace:

Repetition: It strengthens the verbal message by repeating aligned gestures with your words. *For Example*: Nodding your head while saying *"I agree"* reinforces your agreement.

Contradiction: It can contradict your message, signaling to the listener that you may be lying or hiding important details. *For Example*: Saying *"I'm happy for you"* with a subtle frown on your face creates doubt.

Substitution: It substitutes a verbal message by conveying a hidden, vivid feeling through your facial expressions. *For Example*: Offering a warm smile instead of saying *"thank you."*

Complementing: It increases the impact of your message by adding actions to complement your verbal message. *For Example*: Patting someone on the back while praising them for their achievement.

Accenting: It emphasizes and conveys the importance of a verbal message. *For Example*: Pointing to a specific path with your finger while giving directions.

Each part of your body plays a role in showcasing your unique personality. To understand and enhance body language that commands respect, let's first take a quick look at how each body part contributes to the general body language we display when experiencing different emotions.

THE ANATOMY OF PERCEPTION

Eyes: The eyes help signal honesty, attention, or evasion.

Mouth: Smiles can convey warmth and approachability but should always align with the context of the situation.

Hands: Gestures can express confidence in a particular topic, but they should never be exaggerated.

Feet: The directional positioning of your feet reveals your level of interest or disengagement toward the speaker.

Posture: The alignment of your body in a situation demonstrates your presence and readiness.

GENERAL BODY LANGUAGE ACCORDING TO DIFFERENT EMOTIONS

Confidence: When we feel confident, our bodies typically maintain an upright posture with steady eye contact, a focused mind, and relaxed shoulders.

Nervousness: A nervous person may show signs of fidgeting, avoid eye contact, cross their arms while talking, or experience a sense of dizziness.

Anger: Suppressed anger is often signaled through clenched fists, narrowed eyes, or a stiff stance.

Interest: Interested individuals are often slightly leaned forward toward the speaker, maintain engaged eye contact, and nod occasionally to show they are invested in the conversation.

Disinterest: If a person is disinterested in a topic, they may slouch forward or backward, look away frequently, or tap their fingers as a sign of boredom.

MASTERING BODY LANGUAGE THAT COMMANDS RESPECT

Body language is often influenced by an individual's level of comfort. When in close proximity or personal space, if you notice the other person stepping away from your confident stance, it's best to pause and redirect the conversation in a constructive, non-threatening manner. Not everyone is accustomed to handling a strong presence, so it's important to read the other person's behavior and pick up on cues to adjust your approach accordingly.

Practicing your body language in front of a mirror before entering a potentially tense situation will help you stay mindful of the image you want to project.

For example, if you want to be perceived as confident, competent, composed, or comfortable in critical situations, practice the following ten habits in front of a mirror or with a friend.

1. **Stand or sit up straight**. Keep a physical reminder, like a note or digital notification, to remind yourself occasionally to maintain proper posture while standing or sitting.

2. **Keep your head held high**. When walking, focus on a point ahead of you to avoid lowering your neck.

3. **Maintain good posture**. You don't need to spend hours at the gym to improve posture. Simple back stretches, like aligning your back while standing against a wall, can significantly improve your stance. You can also use online resources, such as five-minute yoga stretches, to build a resilient body.

4. **Relax your shoulders**. Straighten your shoulders and keep them relaxed while speaking.

5. **Keep your stance composed**. Distribute your weight evenly on both feet. Avoid leaning on one leg or shifting your weight to one side of your body, unless advised by a physician.

6. **Deliver firm handshakes** to communicate confidence and assurance.

7. **Maintain steady, appropriate eye contact** without staring blankly or intimidatingly.

8. **Stand about two to four feet apart** from the other person to maintain personal space.

9. **Use controlled hand gestures** to emphasize important points during conversation.

10. **Avoid fidgeting**. Focus your mind on an interesting thought or the subject at hand whenever you catch yourself fidgeting or becoming distracted.

FACIAL EXPRESSIONS & TONE OF VOICE

Your face acts as a canvas for your genuine emotions. While skilled manipulators may use facial expressions to deceive others, learning how to master your own facial expressions and tone of voice is crucial for smooth communication during critical situations.

A sincere smile signals openness and willingness to engage, while a furrowed brow often reflects displeasure or confusion about the topic at hand. A clenched jaw can indicate suppressed anger, and a trembling voice may signal nervousness or sadness.

To refine your body language, it's important to work on your facial expressions and tone of voice to respond appropriately to different situations. Both elements are key to presenting a cohesive and authentic image.

Consider practicing the following exercises in front of a mirror or with a friend to improve your facial expressions and tone of voice.

Poker Face: Watch a comical video or one that triggers strong emotions while consciously keeping your facial muscles relaxed and your expressions neutral. This exercise will help you avoid unintentionally revealing emotions in unfavorable situations.

Fake Smile vs. Genuine Smile: Stand in front of a mirror and recall a happy moment. Observe the warm smile you radiate when thinking about it, then try to replicate that smile while imagining work scenarios. Both fake and genuine smiles should be used strategically depending on the situation. A genuine smile typically shows a deep curve with crow's feet around the eyes, while a fake smile does not. However, skilled manipulators can mimic a genuine smile. If you find it difficult to express sincere emotions or your smile feels awkward to others, practice focusing on thoughts that genuinely make you smile.

Expressing Worry or Concern: Many individuals struggle to express negative emotions and tend to resort to a poker face. To show concern in a non-threatening way, practice slightly furrowing your brows or using a warm gaze to appear empathetic without being overdramatic.

The Tone of Your Voice

The tone of your voice can make or break a conversation. For example, if you approach a higher authority for feedback on your recent project and they respond with a grumpy, heavy voice saying, *"There's absolutely nothing worth fixing in your project,"* chances are you'll head back to your desk and spend the entire day looking for potential mistakes in what was otherwise a flawless project.

The casual pace you use when speaking to friends or family should be avoided in a work setting. The more deliberate you are in articulating your words, the more thoughtful you will sound.

In a heated conflict, it's best to respond with a contrasting tone. If you notice the opposing party shouting, use a firm and confident tone to address the issue. This practice can help calm the agitated individual and shift their focus from reacting to the situation to responding to you.

Additionally, be mindful of whether your tone aligns with your words. Sometimes, we sound sad or uninterested when we're genuinely engaged in a conversation. To prevent this, practice maintaining a posture that conveys attentiveness to the speaker.

A tone that is loud, confident, clear, and polite will always help you stand out from the crowd of yellers and whisperers.

SETTING BOUNDARIES WITHOUT BEING IMPOLITE

When you make an effort to set boundaries in the workplace, you are essentially demanding mutual respect and trust from others. Just as skills are essential for landing your dream job, setting boundaries in every aspect of your life is equally important. However, some people may find it offensive when you prioritize your well-being over others. Setting personal boundaries without being impolite requires self-awareness, consistent practice, and adaptability based on the situation. Here's a step-by-step guide to building personal boundaries without offending others.

Identify and Learn About Your Limits: Every individual has a certain threshold for tolerating others' behavior. It's important to recognize which situations, words, or actions trigger you and learn how to manage your emotions in a healthy way. If someone invades your personal space, politely communicate this to them.

For example, if a co-worker or friend invites you to an after-work party, and you're not interested, don't simply agree to keep them company. Instead, explain that you have other plans or personal goals to work on, or simply that you're not in the mood for a crowded place. It's normal to feel drained after work and need some personal time.

Communicate Clearly: Use a firm but polite tone. Rather than confronting your co-worker by accusing them of pressuring you, focus on how you feel and why you want to decline the invitation. A friendly, warm tone will help you express that you're genuinely exhausted and prefer to call it a day.

Non-verbal Reinforcement: Maintain steady eye contact and an open posture to appear less intimidating and non-threatening.

Suggest Alternative Plans: If you feel comfortable, you can propose alternative plans, like: *"Let's check out that new restaurant instead of going to the club"* or *"How about we go shopping this weekend?"* Or, you could suggest, *"Why don't you ask that new co-worker? She was looking for someone to join her at the office party."*

Stay Firm in Your Decisions: Be confident in your choices. Don't waver between options. If necessary, take some time before making a final decision. Frequently changing your mind can make you seem indecisive and make your boundaries appear negotiable. Always restate your boundaries if challenged.

CHAPTER 6: NAVIGATING WORKPLACE MINEFIELDS

Workplaces are often compared to minefields, teeming with dynamic personalities from diverse cultures, backgrounds, opinions, and values. A seemingly harmless word or a casual remark can leave the receiving party feeling threatened or disrespected. Navigating these complex webs of emotions requires more than just competence and likability—it demands thoughtfulness, emotional intelligence, and adaptability, tailored to the receiver's perspective.

In theory, professionalism aims to neutralize such tensions by encouraging individuals to set aside personal emotions and focus on collective goals. However, in reality, power dynamics, bias, and the pressure of high-stakes environments create a daunting gap between this ideal and actual practice. It's not uncommon for higher authorities to reveal their true, often destructive, nature over time, robbing employees of their mental peace.

Whether you are a new hire, an independent contributor, or a top performer at a multinational corporation, navigating workplace minefields is an inevitable part of

your professional journey. Understanding how to face these challenges without compromising your integrity is the key to thriving in any corporate setting. The following subsections will explore practical strategies that you can apply to avoid three common potential minefields in your professional life.

HOW TO AVOID UNNECESSARY CONFLICTS AND MINIMIZE GOSSIP

When a conflict is mismanaged, it can cause significant damage, potentially severing a relationship that could have been beneficial. However, when a conflict is approached and resolved in a respectful and positive manner, it fosters trust and strengthens future connections. There are two primary ways to respond to a conflict: the healthy way and the unhealthy way. Your upbringing can play a role in shaping your initial response to conflict and how you perceive it. However, with patience and practice, you can develop a more positive outlook toward any conflict. Let's first explore the healthy and unhealthy ways of responding to a conflict, as outlined in the Help Guide organization.

HEALTHY RESPONSES	UNHEALTHY RESPONSES
Inability to respond or recognize the matters that are important to the other person.	Showing empathy and working towards finding a collective solution.
Showing explosive nature or using hurtful comments.	A non-defensive attitude and attending to the conflict calmly and respectfully.
Withdrawing yourself from important discussions or when losing the argument.	Showing a readiness to forgive, forget, and move past from harboring resentment.
Uncompromising and Uncooperative.	Showing genuine interest in understanding the other person's perspective or creating a middle ground for both parties.
Feeling scared to confront and expecting a bad outcome.	Being transparent about the challenges and seeking support.

Try to recall this table when you are faced with your next conflict to identify the degree of your initial response. Is it the healthy or positive responses that you first showcase, or is it the negative or unhealthy responses your mind triggers the most? Try to channel your emotions towards the positive sections to avoid unnecessary tension in a conflict or escalating issues. Another effective way to deal with unnecessary conflict is to use humor thoughtfully.

Even if a work setting demands unwavering concentration and seriousness, life isn't all about achieving next month's target. Brush up on your sense of humor and come up with silly, lighthearted responses to ease the tension between you and the other individual. Often, a good laugh is all it takes to melt the dark clouds away.

WORKING BEYOND BUSINESS HOURS

In today's world, the lines between personal and professional life are often blurred due to increased competition. Many individuals sacrifice their personal lives and devote themselves to their work to achieve more, attain greater success, or prove their worth to the world.

Whether you need to respond to emails, stay up late to meet an urgent deadline, or attend untimely meetings for the progression of a project, working beyond business hours takes a serious toll on everyone.

It not only affects your mental and physical well-being but also impacts your overall productivity in other areas of your life. It can lead to burnout, chronic stress, and even serious health risks.

Additionally, always being available to tend to every need of your project or the demands of higher authorities can create an image of a vulnerable, weak person with no personal boundaries. Over time, you may find yourself burdened with unrealistic expectations and trapped in unnecessary, unrewarding tasks.

However, if working late is unavoidable, such as during peak project deadlines or a company crisis, taking a strategic approach can help you avoid being seen as a person with diluted worth. Here are some steps to effectively manage stress and time when dealing with work beyond business hours.

Set Clear Priorities: If assigned a task that may extend your office hours, focus on completing the parts that will yield significant results first, and delegate or attend to the less important ones later.

Approach Them First: If you sense that your manager or co-worker might need your help with a task, approach them first instead of waiting around during your free time. Communicate your preferred working hours to your peers to avoid being pressured into unrealistic expectations.

Take Necessary Breaks: Identify your preferred work method. Some people excel at completing a project in one go and then taking an extended break, while others work more efficiently with short, frequent breaks to avoid monotony. Recognize which approach helps you stay focused and apply it to your work schedule to complete tasks effectively. It's always advisable to take necessary breaks to reduce mistakes and prevent last-minute errors in your project.

Schedule Downtime: After completing a project that requires extended work hours, set aside time to recharge your mind and focus on activities unrelated to work.

Balancing your professional relationships with your commitments makes you more desirable and creates an image of a reliable, determined individual. Maintaining a healthy work-life balance aligns you with favorable opportunities and attracts peers who value quality over quantity.

WHEN TO SEEK EXTERNAL SUPPORT

Challenges in the Workplace: Challenges in the workplace are an essential part of personal and professional growth. However, there are certain situations that reaching out for external support is necessary to protect yourself from life-threatening issues and safeguard your career trajectory.

Harassment: If you experience any form of harassment—be it physical, psychological, or emotional—it's crucial to reach out to higher authorities or employees responsible for handling such matters, such as HR, legal advisors, mentors, or professional counselors. Workplace harassment based on gender, religion, race, personal characteristics, physical appearance, or any factor unrelated to your job performance should be addressed immediately.

Mental Health Issues Due to Excessive Stress: If you are diagnosed with chronic stress, anxiety, or depression and feel overwhelmed, disengaged, or unable to cope with work pressure, consider consulting a mental health counselor to channel your emotions effectively without becoming overburdened.

Unethical Practices: If you witness illegal practices at work, such as fraud, theft, or other unethical behavior, don't turn a blind eye. Seek external support to take immediate action. In some cases, it may be advisable to transfer to a new company rather than continue working under leaders with questionable morals.

Career Stagnation: If you find yourself facing career stagnation despite repeated efforts for growth, it's a good idea to consult a career coach to avoid burnout and redirect your efforts toward achieving your goals.

Financial Discrepancies: If you suspect financial discrepancies or unfair compensation, such as wage theft, unpaid overtime, or altered salary figures, consider consulting labor law experts or external auditors to report any unfair treatment.

Physical or Psychological Safety Concerns: Any threats to your physical or psychological safety within the company—such as a physically abusive boss or co-worker—must be addressed without delay. Legal advisors can help prevent escalation and ensure your safety.

Seeking necessary support is a sign of wisdom, not weakness. When you seek external support, you gain an impartial perspective that not only protects your rights as an employee but also encourages others to speak up when facing unfair treatment.

CHAPTER 7: BUILDING EMOTIONAL STRENGTH AND RESILIENCE

Emotional strength and resilience unlock your true potential to lead a fulfilled and more empowered life. They act as an inner compass to guide you and help you adapt to challenging situations. Understanding how you will feel or react to certain situations and how they will affect your productivity and thoughts in everyday life can be beneficial and often rewarding, as it helps you stay prepared for life's unexpected events.

Emotionally resilient individuals can tackle life's challenges better and practice healthier ways to cope with anxiety and stress. Below is a chart that describes and discusses the five aspects and four components of emotional resilience.

COMPONENT OF EMOTIONAL RESILIENCE	DESCRIPTION	BENEFIT
Self-Awareness	Recognizing The Degree of Your Emotions: Is it positive or negative?	Improves your decision-making abilities
Self-Regulation	Managing Your Emotional Response	Enhances and encourages healthy coping strategies
Empathy	Trying to connect and understand the other party's emotions	Strengthens interpersonal relationships and expands your networking skills
Adaptability	Being open and flexible to change	Helps in overcoming challenges smoothly

ASPECT	EMOTIONALLY RESILIENT INDIVIDUALS	LESS EMOTIONALLY RESILIENT INDIVIDUALS
Stress Level	Low	High
Adaptability	High	Low
Seeking Support	Proactive	Avoidant
Coping Strategies	Healthy	Unhealthy
Interpersonal Relationships	Strong	Weak

If you find yourself more aligned with less resilient individuals or wish to solidify your emotional strength and resilience, you must first consider making changes in your daily habits. The next subsection explores the myriad benefits of practicing healthy personal habits and how they influence your work life.

HOW PERSONAL HABITS INFLUENCE YOUR WORK LIFE

Your habits are interconnected with your professional life. If you are a person who is active and likes to maintain a certain order in your household responsibilities, chances are you often demonstrate similar habits in your workplace, such as maintaining project deadlines or keeping your desk organized.

Every person shows traits of their daily habits in their work life. Suppose someone says they are lazy at handling personal affairs but you observe them being efficient at every professional activity. In that case, they are likely just less self-aware of their habits at home. If a person regularly maintains a routine schedule at home, they will likely unconsciously follow a structured work routine. Your daily habits boost your morale and enhance your ability to deal with stress during tough times.

The sought-after productivity trends or routines such as the 1-week glow challenge, winter arc, or ghost mode that you often encounter on your social media feed mostly involve steps to transform your mindset and outlook toward life. Whether following a 75-day hard challenge or preparing a 90-day social media growth calendar, consistency and a strategic approach are the keys to achieving your goals and changing your life dynamically.

You need to sit down and write your thoughts every single day to become better at articulation. You need to read and learn voraciously to become a better speaker. You need to go to the gym and follow a 3-day workout routine to achieve significant results, and you need to keep showing up every day for opportunities to eventually find you.

Incorporating mindful activities and exercises into your daily routine enhances your emotional resilience toward personal and professional affairs and also brings long-term benefits for your overall well-being.

Here are five detailed charts that showcase the benefits of daily habits and how they help you become an emotionally resilient individual.

HABITS TO PRACTICE REGULARLY

HABIT	BENEFIT
Meditation	Boost Focus and Concentration
Regular Physical Activity or Exercise	Enhances Mood and Reduces Anxiety
Gratitude Journal	Helps To Shift Your Focus and Build a Positive Solution Oriented Outlook Towards Life
Connecting With Supporting Social Networks	Refines Your Networking Skills
Trying Tasks That Force You to Step Out of Your Comfort Zone	Make Challenges and Change Less Daunting and Help You to Adapt Accordingly

COPING STRATEGIES FOR COMMON TRIGGERS OF STRESS

STRESS TRIGGER	IDENTIFICATION	COPING STRATEGY
Deadlines	Track Task Completion	Apply Time Management Techniques
Interpersonal Relationships	Identify The Main Triggers Causing the Conflict	Open Communication and Strategic Approach

Financial Concerns	Track Budget	Consult Financial Advice
Health Issues	Regular Health Checkup	Healthy Lifestyle Choices. Start with a small change like taking the stairs 3 times a week instead of the elevator.
Major Life Challenges	Reflect On Significant Shifts	Plan For the Future, Reach Out for Help and Seek Guidance

FREQUENCY AND PURPOSE OF EACH HABIT

HABIT	PURPOSE	FREQUENCY
Journaling	Self- Reflection	Daily
Speech Practice / Role Playing	Build Confidence and Help in Better Articulation of Thoughts	Weekly
Yoga/ Walking / Running/ Swimming/ Gym/ Pilates any form of exercise that makes your heart pump up more oxygen	Stress Relief, Improved Posture, and Good Health	3 to 4 times a week

SELF-CARE STRATEGIES AND ITS EFFECT ON RESILIENCE BUILDING & MENTAL HEALTH

Self-Care Strategies	Mental Health Benefits	Effect On Resilience Building
Regular Exercise	Reduces Anxiety and Improves Mood	Enhances Healthy Coping Mechanisms and Thoughts

Setting Boundaries	Boost Self-esteem and Self-worth	Encourages Emotional Safety
Leisure Activities or Hobbies	Relax And Recharge Your Mind	Fosters Adaptability
Mindful Practices	Increases Self-awareness and Presence	Builds Emotional Control

BENEFITS OF PRACTICING DAILY GRATITUDE

Mental Health Aspect	Benefit Of Practicing Daily Gratitude
Anxiety	Reduction In Anxiety and Stress by Shifting Your Focus on Positive Experiences
Mood	Significant Improvement in Mood Through Daily Reflection
Resilience	Enhances Ability to Cope with Stress and Adversity
Interpersonal Relationship	Strengthens Bonds by Improving Networking Skills

Self-care routines and nurturing a positive mindset are crucial aspects of emotional resilience as they help prepare your mind to regulate stress during unfavorable conditions. These practices also help in shaping a dynamic personality and make you a magnet for opportunities and growth.

HOW TO BECOME A GOOD LISTENER

As our society advances toward becoming an AI-driven community, many find themselves engaging in meaningful conversations with AI rather than with other humans around them. Employers who lack active listening skills often experience the highest turnover rates among top performers.

Active listening is a key component of leadership. If you want to become a great leader, be a better listener first. If you want to become a famous orator, listen to better dialogues. Listening is the most vital life skill that is sadly undertaught. Every person on this planet carries an unspoken wish to have someone who will make them feel heard, but very few of us consciously make efforts to become a better listener for others.

Conversations in workplaces often become battlefields where almost every participant treats active listening as transactional—given only when there's a personal agenda to fulfill or a benefit to reap.

Active listening is a two-way gift that benefits both the listener and the speaker. It helps you refine your leadership qualities, your networking abilities, and enhances your problem-solving skills. To become a better listener at work, start by practicing this quick exercise at home.

Practice Exercise

Choose a TED talk, an award speech, a standup comedy performance, a chat show, or a book that you enjoy. Once you are satisfied with your selection, listen to the entire video or read each part of the book attentively. Afterward, switch off the screen or close the book and try to recall aloud the topics discussed in the video or chapter. Make it as detailed as you can without using any physical tools. Rely solely on your mind and ears; if needed, you can rewatch the same content multiple times until you have a solid grasp of the topics discussed. You don't necessarily have to understand everything shared in the content, just make sure to touch on every point when you recall it.

This is a beneficial exercise for improving your active listening skills as it targets your memory, thought articulation, speech, and listening capacity simultaneously. The reason I suggest not using physical tools such as a notepad or pen is that in real-life conversations, we rarely have the chance to pull out a notebook and make bullet points about what the speaker is trying to convey. Practicing this exercise regularly will also improve your focus and help you be fully present in the moment.

Honing your listening skills will transform people's perceptions of you. At work, you will be recognized as someone who possesses strong leadership traits and solves problems quickly and effectively by making each team member feel seen and heard.

Here is a quick list for you to become a better listener:

Avoid Interruption: Use small verbal cues to acknowledge and encourage the speaker, such as a nod or saying *"That makes sense"* or *"Go on, I'm listening."* Don't interrupt them to share your views; let them complete.

Use Thoughtful Phrases: Stop reacting to issues with phrases like *"that's bad,"* *"Wish I could do something to help,"* or *"I feel your pain."* Instead, use thoughtful, empathetic responses such as *"What steps are you taking to cope with the issue so far?"* or *"Is there any vital lesson you learned from this?"* or *"What changes did you see in yourself after dealing with this specific incident?"*

Read The Person: Sometimes people just need someone to listen while they vent, not solutions. In such cases, just be a friendly listener to help the person regulate their emotions by themselves.

Listening is a currency that is exchanged between the speaker and the listener. In real-life conversations, when you choose to listen to someone, don't just listen to remember their words or provide solutions; try to understand the real meaning and motive behind the stories they share.

HOW TO CREATE A FAVORABLE OPPORTUNITY

In the workplace, you cannot dictate or alter how someone behaves toward you, but you do hold complete power over how you would like to respond to their actions and words. When faced with a critical situation, your response determines whether you will make the outcome

favorable or unfavorable to your growth.

Opportunities can knock even under the direst of circumstances.

While many authentic leaders advocate this perspective, few provide tangible steps to seize these opportunities. In my view, opportunities are subjective to the receiver's perspective. What feels like a golden chance to one individual might turn into a hidden trap for another. So, when you consider seizing opportunities for your growth, you must always take note of your unique traits, strengths, and weaknesses.

There are several practical ways that serve as a blueprint to transform unfavorable circumstances into aligned opportunities; however, a quick SWOT analysis could come in handy before committing to building the stepping stones for your success.

HOW TO CONDUCT S.W.O.T ANALYSIS

The SWOT analysis framework is typically used to evaluate a company's competitive position in a business sector. It involves steps that carefully analyze and assess both internal and external factors, as well as the company's current and future potential.

The abbreviation SWOT stands for:

S: Strengths

W: Weaknesses

O: Opportunities

T: Threats

This technique is designed to facilitate a realistic, fact-based, data-driven look at the core strengths and potential weaknesses of an initiative, organization, or industry. Here are the steps to effectively implement a SWOT analysis in identifying the internal and external factors that influence your growth and productivity.

Step 1: Take a piece of paper or open your digital notepad.

Step 2: Analyze Your Strengths.

Ask yourself the following questions:

• What are my interests and skills?

• Are there any achievements that I'm proud of?

• What qualities in me do others consistently praise me for?

Action Tip: List all your skills, qualifications, accomplishments, and personality traits. Cross-check with people who provide you with genuine feedback such as mentors, peers, and colleagues.

Step 3: Analyze Your Weaknesses

Ask yourself the following questions:

• What tasks or skills do I struggle with the most?

• What habits or behaviors are holding me back?

• Is there any specific fear associated with past failures?

Action Tip: Focus on recurring patterns or challenges that undermine your optimal performance. Seek constructive criticism for a better viewpoint.

Step 4: Explore Opportunities

Questions to ask yourself:

• What are the current trends and updates in my field that could fuel my growth?

• Any new skills or knowledge that will boost my career growth?

• Who in my network could help me align and unlock new opportunities?

Action Tip: Keep yourself updated and well-informed by attending workshops, networking events, and learning about new trends or applications.

Step 5: Acknowledge Threats

Ask yourself the following questions:

• What external factors or responsibilities could negatively impact my growth?

• Who or what poses competition in my personal and professional growth?

• Are there any social, economic, or geographical risks that I must consider?

Action Tip: Develop backup plans for unexpected challenges. Keep your solutions flexible to reduce the impact of any unavoidable circumstances or damage.

Creating opportunities from unfavorable circumstances acts as an invitation for creative solutions. Once you are done with a quick S.W.OT. Analysis, scanning your entire personality, habits, and key traits, it's time to dedicate yourself to the art of creating favorable circumstances. Here are six detailed strategies to help you get started on your journey.

STRATEGY I

Ask open-ended questions that begin with *"How Might We?"*

For example: How might we help a colleague finish their task on time to avoid delaying the submission of the project?

STRATEGY II

Shift your focus to the root of the problem and build your solutions around it to eliminate the cause once and for all.

For Example: Instead of finding ways to tackle or avoid your angry boss or supervisor, identify the root cause of their frustration.

STRATEGY III

Avoid solution bias. Keep opportunities free of pre-defined solutions to encourage innovative approaches.

For Example: If you are trying to solve a conflict in a group discussion, avoid stating general solutions right at the beginning of the discussion and let each member craft their unique solutions.

STRATEGY IV

When you let team members expand the scope of solutions, you also risk diverting the focus from the root issue. Keep the discussion focused on solving the root problem. **For Example:** When you catch your team or yourself being diverted from the main topic, immediately ask *'How may we link the (specific topic) to deal with the current problem.'*

STRATEGY V

Try to use positive phrasing throughout conversations to increase the chances of finding a wider range of creative solutions. **For Example:** Instead of saying *'How may we reduce errors in our processes?'* say *'How may we keep our teams more informed of the new processes?'*

STRATEGY VI

When you create several opportunities from your crisis, make sure that each one of them contributes to a comprehensive list to boost your career. Try to avoid overlapping the timeline of opportunities and keep them exclusive according to their priority.

CHAPTER 8: HOW TO RECLAIM YOUR POWER FROM NARCISSISTS & MANIPULATORS.

Narcissism is a complex personality disorder in which the person struggles to consider the needs of others. You can easily spot a narcissist in a crowd when you see someone with an inflated sense of self and a fragile ego, often rambling about their achievements or problems. Every conversation they have is filled with "I" statements, and their sole motive is to prove they are superior to everyone around them. Narcissists and manipulators often exhibit similar habits and personality traits.

Reclaiming your sanity from the grip of a narcissist or manipulator is challenging but not impossible. To heal from the exploitative behaviors of a narcissist, you must first learn to detach your emotions from them and the words they use to interact with you.

Recognize the need for change to stay motivated and avoid falling into the cycle of

negative remarks. When you become self-aware of your strengths and weaknesses and value your self-worth, it's unlikely a narcissist will trap you in their web.

Assessing the impact of your emotions is just as important, as it can often lead to confusion and troubling thoughts. Learn to forgive yourself for past mistakes, as mistakes are what help us grow as individuals. Prioritize your well-being by reclaiming your power from narcissists and manipulators in your professional life.

CONCLUSION

Now that you've finished reading this book, I hope it has helped you see manipulators and narcissists in a new light. They are people too, flawed like the rest of us. While it is always wise to avoid them (I mean, by all means, RUN if you have the option!), facing them can transform you as an individual. It's not the external storm created by others that we need to deal with, but the chaos we allow ourselves to go through after facing the storm.

Learning to deal with difficult people is much like trying to impress that one high school teacher who seemed to hold a grudge against you for no particular reason. It will always require a great amount of patience, strategy, and resilience.

When I started researching for this book, I gained invaluable insights from skilled writers, which are often discussed in the chapters. Their perspectives on workplace archetypes and leadership have shaped my own view in a deeply influential way.

Many of the practices in this guide are methods I developed myself when I started working independently. These techniques now serve as a compass for my new projects. I hope they help you tackle life's challenges with bravery and inspire new, creative ways to deal with the difficult people you may encounter.

Final Reflections

The reason I incorporated daily habits into this guide is that maintaining healthy personal practices helps drive away fatigue and boredom. The strategies, techniques, useful phrases, and effective methods discussed throughout this book are meaningless if you continue letting difficult people dictate your growth. Life is too short to focus on changing the behaviors of others toward you. Instead, focus on empowering yourself to radiate joy and uplift those around you.

Self-help books like this are incredibly beneficial when you understand that your mental well-being defines your worth, not your paycheck.

Navigating the complexities of interpersonal relationships and consistently learning the fine art of dealing with difficult people will make your life fulfilling, peaceful, and abundant.

Thank you for taking the time to read this book. Your work is just one part of the rich tapestry that makes up your life. It is your mindset, resilience, and the courage you show while embracing life's challenges that truly define your worth. ***You are so much more than your circumstances.***

CHEAT SHEET

1. The key to building strong interpersonal relationships is learning how to balance assertiveness with kindness.

2. Identify the key archetype of the manipulator to equip yourself with unshakable and firm boundaries.

3. Spot inconsistencies in behavior and words to encourage accountability.

4. Recognize your unique work triggers so you can adopt proactive strategies and resolve conflicts faster.

5. Approach heated conflicts with a calm and confident demeanor.

6. Encourage discussion of open-ended topics during cold conflicts.

7. Practice role-playing in front of the mirror to improve your ability to articulate your thoughts.

8. Prioritize breaks and completely disconnect your mind to avoid burnout.

9. Reach out for external help when necessary.

10. Ask questions to understand the person's point of view, rather than solely focusing on solving the problem.

11. Build healthy habits at home—start with one small habit at a time.

Jacqueline D. Austin

Printed in Great Britain
by Amazon

57685619R00057